Cold War
and
Coexistence

Prentice-Hall

America's Role in World Affairs Series

Dankwart A. Rustow, Editor

RUPERT EMERSON
Africa and United States Policy

WALTER GOLDSTEIN
Military Strategy in World Politics

WILLIAM E. GRIFFITH
Cold War and Coexistence: Russia, China, and the United States

ERNST B. HAAS
The Web of Interdependence: The United States
and International Organizations

M. DONALD HANCOCK and DANKWART A. RUSTOW, eds.
American Foreign Policy in International Perspective

STANLEY HOFFMANN
Europe and United States Policy

CHARLES BURTON MARSHALL
The Burden of Decision: American Foreign Policy Since 1945

JOHN D. MONTGOMERY
Foreign Aid in International Politics

WILLIAM C. OLSON
The Making of United States Foreign Policy

DANKWART A. RUSTOW
The New Setting of World Politics

KALMAN H. SILVERT
Latin America and United States Policy

WAYNE A. WILCOX
Asia and United States Policy

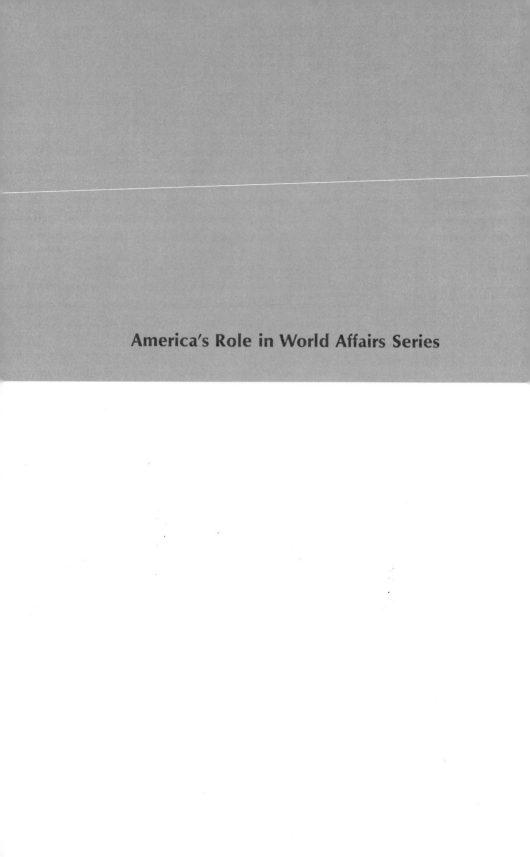

America's Role in World Affairs Series

WILLIAM E. GRIFFITH
Massachusetts Institute of Technology

Cold War
and
Coexistence

Russia, China, and the United States

PRENTICE-HALL, INC., ENGLEWOOD CLIFFS, N.J.

C-13-139626-9
P-13-139618-8

Current printing (last number):
10   9   8   7   6   5   4   3   2   1

PRENTICE-HALL INTERNATIONAL, INC. *London*
PRENTICE-HALL OF AUSTRALIA, PTY. LTD. *Sydney*
PRENTICE-HALL OF CANADA, LTD. *Toronto*
PRENTICE-HALL OF INDIA PRIVATE LTD. *New Delhi*
PRENTICE-HALL OF JAPAN, INC. *Tokyo*

America's Role in
World Affairs Series

Specialized knowledge and practical experience combine
to lay the solid foundations for this survey of AMERICA'S
ROLE IN WORLD AFFAIRS. Eleven distinguished authors
distill their insights, refined in years spent as responsible government officials, as high-level advisers to governments, in
prolonged field research, and in teaching at our leading uni-
versities. Their volumes emphasize the lasting realities under-
lying current conflict, the political forces in the present that
will shape the world of the future. Separately, each volume in
the series is a concise, authoritative analysis of a problem area
of major significance. Taken as a whole, the series gives a
broader and more diversified coverage than would be possible
in a single book on American foreign policy and international
relations.

An introductory volume by the series editor appraises
the rapidly changing environment of foreign policy in the
second half of the twentieth century—the revolution of modernization, the multiplication of sovereign states, and the

tightening network of communication around the globe. In bold and deft strokes, William C. Olson analyzes the forces of public opinion, congressional action, and planning and implementation in the executive branch that combine to shape American foreign policy. Charles Burton Marshall takes the reader to the inner councils of United States policy as he retraces with wit, urbanity, and a lively sense of drama some of the crucial turning points in our foreign relations.

Three volumes deal systematically with some of the major instruments of contemporary foreign policy. Walter Goldstein cogently links the breathless pace of military technology in a nuclear age to some of the perennial dimensions of human conflict and strategic calculation. The wide range of uses—the possibilities and limitations—of foreign aid yield to John D. Montgomery's penetrating treatment. Ernst B. Haas combines sober realism with a passionate sense of human interdependence in his succinct account of the contemporary pattern of international organization.

Another group of volumes takes us to regions where the drama of modern international politics is being enacted. The intimate and yet often frustrating relations between the United States and Western Europe are sharply illuminated by Stanley Hoffmann's irony and subtle understanding. William E. Griffith clarifies the awesome issues of Cold War and coexistence in the triangular relations among the United States, the Soviet Union, and Communist China. Wayne Ayres Wilcox, in a synthesis of rare breadth and depth, allows the reader to grasp the full complexities of that geographic concept called Asia. The problems of new states, with their bitter memories of the colonial past and their ardent hopes for a better future, are presented with sympathy and skepticism in Rupert Emerson's volume on Africa. Kalman H. Silvert draws on two decades of travel and study and on his keen sense for the explosive issues of evolution vs. revolution as he sums up the record of our relations with Latin America.

The contributors have sought no consensus of policy preference and no narrow uniformity of scholarly method. They share a conviction that policy must operate within a context of circumstance that allows now a wider, now a narrower, choice of alternatives and that sound policy must be formulated from a thorough knowledge of that context. They hold that valid theory in the social sciences must rise upon solid empirical foundations. They also believe that clarity and conciseness do not detract from true scholarship but, on the contrary, enhance it. Within such broad assumptions, each author has applied his specialized knowledge and his practical experience to one distinctive facet of AMERICA'S ROLE IN WORLD AFFAIRS.

DANKWART A. RUSTOW

Contents

Introduction

Before the outbreak in July 1914 of World War I, *the*
great watershed of modern history, few except Alexis de Tocqueville would have thought that fifty years later world
politics would be dominated by the relations among the
United States, Russia, and China. The United States then
still deliberately played only a peripheral role in international
politics. The Soviet Union did not yet exist; and its prede-
cessor, the Russian Empire, was underdeveloped, weakened
from its defeat by the Japanese in 1905, and menaced by the
rising power of Imperial Germany. The Chinese Empire,
whose power had been steadily declining for a century, had
just collapsed. China, almost a colony of the Western imperialist powers, seemed weaker than ever. World politics centered in Europe, as it had for centuries; and Great Britain,
France, and Imperial Germany were still the most powerful
countries in the world.

Since 1914 the two world wars have wrought an enormous and, it seems increasingly likely, a permanent revolution in international politics. True, Western Europe has recovered from its 1945 near-collapse. Germany lost both world wars and since 1945 has been divided. Yet, West Germany is now the third and East Germany the eighth industrial nation in the world. However, West European recovery has been cast far into the shade by the enormous growth in the economic, technological, and, above all, military power of the United States and—albeit to a somewhat lesser extent—of the Soviet Union. Only these two powers have the population, the territory, and the natural resources to be continental powers; and the rush forward of modern technology makes it increasingly clear that only continental powers can hope to play genuinely independent roles in world affairs. Moreover, only the United States and Russia are atomic superpowers; that is, only they have the power to destroy each other and the rest of the world. Added to that, the newest developments in nuclear weapons, multiple warhead missiles (MIRV), and anti-ballistic missile (ABM) systems, which probably only they will deploy, make them militarily even more superior to the other, smaller powers.

China is only *potentially* a superpower. Its more than seven hundred million people are in some respects—for example, the frequent necessity to buy grain abroad to feed them—more of a liability than an asset. It still has far to go to become an industrialized power. Japan, one of the major developed nations of the world, and economically and politically the most promising candidate to be the third superpower, could soon surpass it militarily and is far ahead of it in other respects. The disorders attendant upon China's Cultural Revolution have continued to cast doubt on the unity and effectiveness of its central government. Even so, China, one of the world's great powers for most of the three thousand years of its existence, is in the long run on the rise again. Its defeat of India in the Himalayan frontier skirmish of 1962, its standoff with the United States in the Korean War, its atomic capacity, and the expansionism of its rulers make it one of the major regional powers in Asia, and thereby one whose interests directly involve the United States and Russia in their roles as Asian as well as worldwide powers.

The fundamental political and military pattern of our present world, and in all probability of the near future, was shaped in one decade, from 1939 to 1949. During those ten years World War II destroyed the central position of Europe in world politics, made the United States the major world power, extended the power of Russia into central and eastern Europe and made it the other world power, and brought atomic capacity first to Washington and then to Moscow. The victory of the Chinese Communists in 1949 meant that for the first time since the eighteenth century China would again be unified, would have a strong government, and would attempt to resume its traditional role as the dominating power of east and southeast Asia.

Since 1949 four other major events have occurred. The first was the industrial recovery of Western Europe and Japan, which, however, in neither case has at least as yet been accompanied by an equivalent increase in political and military power, because of West European disunity and Japanese abstention. The second was the Sino-Soviet split, which was foreshadowed in the 1950's and had become, as we now know, probably irreparable by the end of that decade. The third was the constant rise since 1961 of the economic, technological, and military power of the United States, confirming its position as the most powerful nation in the world. The fourth, and most recent, has been the growing internal problems of both superpowers; racial and student discontent in the United States, intellectual and nationalities discontent in Russia.

There have been, of course, other important developments: the Berlin crisis; the Korean War; the Cuban missile

crisis of 1962—*the* watershed of postwar politics; and the
Vietnam War. Together, these form the framework of postwar
politics; and they all center around the rivalries of three
powers, the United States, Russia and the Chinese People's
Republic—the subject of this book.

1

The United States and Russia in Modern History

Until 1945 Russia and the United States remained powers in the wings, facing the center of world politics—Europe. Thereafter, for the first time in centuries, Europe became an object, not the center, of politics; and the conflict between Washington and Moscow has since dominated world affairs.

"Her Majesty's Government," the nineteenth-century British Prime Minister Lord Palmerston remarked, "has neither permanent friends nor permanent enemies but only permanent interests." Imperial Russia carried out its foreign policy according to this maxim; and so, in spite of its often moralistic rhetoric, did the United States. The key to Russian-American relations until 1917 was that both states felt themselves menaced by the same powers and were therefore inclined to support each other: in the nineteenth century by Great Britain, the dominant power at that time; and in the twentieth century, far more sharply, by Germany and Japan.

SIMILARITIES AND DIFFERENCES

Both Russia and the United States are continental powers, with large land areas and natural resources. They have also been, as nations go, relatively saturated; that is, they had already expanded to the Pacific and had so much to do at home that they were relatively less interested in further expansion. This was perhaps truer of the United States than of Russia, whose western frontier was open to invasion, and who was, therefore, constantly preoccupied with its defense. But basically it was true of both: they possessed so much that the basic purpose of their foreign policies was to guard, preserve, and develop what they had.

Furthermore, both were frontier nations—daughters, rather than original participants, of European culture. Russians and Americans, therefore, both shared an energy, a sense of wide spaces and open horizons, a friendliness and hospitality, and a feeling that their nations were greater, more powerful, and not least, more virtuous than any others.

They both had, in other words, a sense of "manifest destiny, of a great future." Farseeing Europeans have long realized this. The great French political philosopher Alexis de Tocqueville wrote more than a century ago:

> There are at present two great nations in the world which seem to tend toward the same end, although they start from different points. I allude to the Russians and the Americans. . . . Each of them appears to be marked by the will of heaven to sway the destinies of half the globe.

Yet, with all their similarities, Russia and the United States have always been vastly different from each other. American culture has been predominantly Protestant and Anglo-Saxon; Russian, Byzantine and Russian Orthodox. When liberalism and democracy were developing in America's motherland, England, the Mongols tyrannized over the conquered Russians. Russia had neither Renaissance nor Reformation; and its modernization, as exemplified by Tsar Peter the Great, was characterized not by democratization, as in England, but by the imposition of an oppressive, highly centralized, bureaucratic autocracy, first under the Tsars, the "Autocrats of All the Russias," and then under the Bolsheviks.

RUSSIAN-AMERICAN RELATIONS

Until Russia and the United States confronted each other directly for power in the world, at the end of World War II, their relations reflected this basic contradiction between the similarity of their state interests (of uniting against their mutual opponents and enemies) and the contrast of their political philosophies and political and social systems.

Until the late nineteenth century, the first characteristic —the similarity of state interests—was dominant. This was essentially so because the Russian autocracy did not feel itself seriously menaced by democratic tendencies and, even more, because the United States was still so weak and so desirous of being left alone, so content, indeed, in its "splendid isolation," that its dislike of Russian oppression was not seriously reflected in its foreign policies.

During the early history of the United States, Great Britain was the leading world power, and both Washington and St. Petersburg, fearing British maritime predominance, tended to support each other against it. In the Revolutionary War, the Russian Empress Catherine refused to aid Great Britain against its rebellious colonists. Tsar Alexander I tried to mediate, in American favor, in the War of 1812, in order to prevent the United States from aligning itself with an even greater danger to Russia—Napoleon. Thomas Jefferson and Alexander I carried on a cordial correspondence, and John Quincy Adams, the first United States minister at St. Petersburg, firmly established Russian-American friendship.

Russian-American common interests were sufficiently

strong to survive some strains in the first half of the nineteenth century. President Monroe's Doctrine, which in 1823 barred the Americas from any additional European colonization, was caused not only by fear that the Holy Alliance, led by Tsar Alexander I, would try to regain Spain's Latin-American colonies for her, but also by American concern about Russian expansion down the Pacific Coast from its Alaskan colony. (Actually, Russia had already decided not to expand farther south.) Moreover, the brutal Tsarist suppression of the Polish revolts in 1830 and 1863 and the Hungarian revolt in 1848 made Russia more unpopular in the United States. Even so, Washington sympathized with Russia in the Crimean War.

The outbreak of the Civil War brought Russian-American friendship to its greatest height until World War I. As Secretary of State Seward wrote:

> Russia . . . has our friendship, in preference to any other European power, simply because she always wishes us well, and leaves us to conduct our affairs as we think best.

Russia's policy favored the North because, as before, the Russians felt they needed a powerful United States to counterbalance British naval supremacy. St. Petersburg, therefore, strongly and consistently opposed British and French efforts to mediate or to aid the South. Pro-Russian sentiment in the American North, already favorably predisposed to Tsar Alexander II as a result of his liberation of the serfs—so parallel in time and action to Lincoln's freeing of the slaves—reached a new height as a result of the "goodwill" visit in 1863 of Russian naval squadrons to New York and San Francisco. (Actually, historical research revealed much later that Alexander had sent the ships there because he feared a war with England and France and knew that if that happened his navy would be either destroyed or blockaded. But very few Americans guessed that at the time, and American gratitude to the Tsar, for what they saw as a demonstration in favor of the Union, was great.)

Shortly after the Civil War, in 1867, the one great potential territorial source of conflict between the United States and Russia was removed when Russia sold Alaska to the United States for $7.2 million. St. Petersburg decided to sell Alaska because the sea otter trade there was no longer profitable, and because, as the Anglo-French naval bombardment of the Russian far eastern port of Petropavlovsk during the Crimean War had demonstrated, Russia could not defend Alaska anyway if war were to break out. Secretary Seward, an impassioned imperialist, finally succeeded in persuading a reluctant Congress to buy what was then called Seward's Folly, with some assistance in the form of bribes to leading Congressmen by the Russian minister in Washington.

Decline in the Nineteenth Century

After this peak in Russian-American friendship, a decline set in during the last decades of the nineteenth century. This had two causes: the first, and less important, was the unfavorable impact on American public opinion of the Tsarist persecution of the Jews, notably the bloody pogroms against them. (Millions of them fled to the United States and greatly reinforced American anti-Russian sentiments.) This led in 1912 to Congress forcing President Taft to terminate the Russo-American trade treaty. The second, more important but more temporary, was the growth of Russian and American rivalry with respect to China, where Russia was pushing south and the United States wanted to maintain the Open Door in order to safeguard its commercial interests.

The late nineteenth century was an imperial age, and both Russia and the United States were infected by its virus. Russia wanted Manchuria and predominant influence in China; America had kept the Philippines and was determined to maintain its trading access to China. Tension between the two countries became so great that when the Russo-Japanese War broke out in 1905, most Americans favored the Japanese. However, President Theodore Roosevelt, determined to keep a balance of power in the Far East in order to safeguard U.S. interests there, and aware of rising Japanese power, mediated in such a fashion that Russia suffered less than it might have. But fundamentally, by replacing Russia in Manchuria, Japan had won the war; and from then on until 1945, Japan, not Russia, was the main menace to the balance of power in East Asia. Tokyo, therefore, and no longer St. Petersburg, became the subject of the main American concern in the Far East, which thereupon ceased to be an obstacle to Russo-American relations until the end of World War II. Moreover, Britain, threatened by Germany, improved its relations with both Russia and the United States, thus removing the shared anti-British basis of Russo-American good relations.

The Rise of Lenin

From the beginning of World War I, most Americans sided with the Allies (Britain, Russia, and France) against the Central Powers (Germany and Austria-Hungary), both because of America's traditional and political sympathies with the Western democracies and because a German victory would have meant domination of the European continent by one single power, something to which American (like British) interests have always been opposed. But American sympathies with Russia were restrained by dislike for Tsarist autocracy. When Tsar Nicholas II was overthrown in February 1917 by a democratic revolution, this obstacle was removed, and Russian-American relations reached the greatest cordiality they ever achieved, before or since. Allies in war and now both democracies—in this situation, American enthusiasm, official and public, knew no bounds.

The greater was the shock for the United States, therefore, when a few months thereafter Lenin and his Bolsheviks came to power. Ideology joined national interests to make the Bolsheviks repugnant to the United States: they were atheistic, Communist, repressive—everything that most Americans hated. Even worse, they took Russia out of the war against

Germany, just as American troops were going into the lines in France. (Indeed, many Americans, including the then American Ambassador in Russia, were—mistakenly—convinced that Lenin and the Bolsheviks were German agents.)

American Interventions

There then ensued one of the most blundering episodes in American foreign policy, the aftermath of which has poisoned Soviet-American relations ever since: the American interventions in the last stages of World War I in northern Russia, at Archangel, and in the Russian Far Eastern Provinces, at Vladivostok. The prime movers in these interventions were not the Americans, but the British and even more the French. President Wilson intervened most reluctantly and for reasons which, although mistaken, were not primarily anti-Communist.

The primary purpose of intervention was initially to revive Russian resistance to the Germans, and only secondarily and thereafter, particularly on the part of the British, to aid the various Russian anti-Communist groups to overthrow Lenin and the Bolsheviks. The interventions were not major in character and were badly mishandled in practice. They were not, in spite of Russian allegations to the effect, primarily a part of a vast "capitalist plot" to overthrow the Soviet regime. But the interventions were "worse than a crime, a blunder." They played into the Bolsheviks' hands and achieved the worst of both worlds: they accomplished none of their objectives and made Soviet antagonism to the West in general, and to America in particular, even worse than it might otherwise have been. Lenin won the civil war in Russia because he realized that his country was sick of the war and determined to get out of it. And he did just that because of the divisions and incompetence of his Russian anti-Communist opponents, and because of the halfheartedness, incompetence, and bungling of the West.

THE POLICIES OF LENIN AND STALIN

Soviet hostility to the West would have been great and essentially unyielding in any case. Lenin was not a Russian nationalist; on the contrary, he was a genuine internationalist and consciously guided himself by what to him seemed the demands of the international proletarian revolution. Like all socialists, before the war he had thought of Germany as the center of the socialist movement, and he was convinced that the success of a Communist revolution there, to which he looked forward with optimism, would shift the center of the world revolution from Moscow to Berlin. The great majority of his senior associates shared these views.

But Lenin was, above all, a political pragmatist with respect to preserving and extending the Communist revolution. When he came to power he overrode the romantic revolutionary impulses of many of his associates and in 1917 made peace with the Germans at Brest-Litovsk, even at the price of ceding much territory. When in 1919 the Communist revolt failed in Germany and in 1920 the Red Army was checked at the Vistula by the Poles, Lenin ruthlessly and realistically adjusted to a long period of "encirclement by capitalism"; that is, of communism being in power only in Russia, with the rest of the world remaining hostile to it and, therefore, toward the identification of the world Communist revolution with the interests of the Soviet state. (He also introduced liberalization in domestic affairs—the New Economic Policy, NEP, which gave more leeway to small-scale private enterprise.)

Stalin's foreign policies were fundamentally the same. Like Lenin, he remained devoted to the strategic goal of world revolution and therefore, since Russia was the only Communist state, to the maintenance and expansion of Soviet power. But unlike Lenin, he knew little of the outside world, and he profoundly feared and distrusted it. A Georgian by birth, he became a fervent Great Russian nationalist and kept the other Soviet nationalities (41 percent of the U.S.S.R.'s population) under domination by Great Russians. Moreover, his bloody purges at home were accompanied by similar methods abroad, as his attack on Finland and policies in eastern Poland (as carried out by his lieutenant, Khrushchev) demonstrated in 1939. In brief, what for Lenin was an inevitable but regrettable equating of Russian national interests with those of the world revolution became for Stalin a total merging of the two, with the accent in reality on the former.

Since for two decades communism, with the minor exception of Outer Mongolia, remained confined to Russia, the Soviet Communist party was much stronger than the other Communist parties throughout the world and, therefore, inevitably became their master. Nor did Lenin hesitate to enforce, however, diplomatically, this natural predominance. Stalin, consumed with neurotic suspicion of his foreign as well as of his domestic associates, went much further: he first enforced rigid and total subordination of all Communist party leaderships to his policies, and after the mid-1930 s he ruthlessly purged their leaderships, killing many, imprisoning more, and turning those left into powerless puppets who danced to his tune. (In all fairness to him, it must be added that he did even worse things to his own Russian party associates; his slaughter of them after 1935 was enormous.)

In foreign affairs, Lenin and Stalin after him had two priorities; first, to consolidate their base at home; second, and thereafter, to expand Communist—and therefore Russian—influence abroad. Stalin was prepared to go to much greater —and bloodier—lengths than Lenin in this, both in repression at home, on which he built the Soviet industrial base, and, starting in 1939, in similar repression abroad. Once World War I was over, the anti-Communist forces had been defeated, and foreign interventions ceased, the Bolsheviks' first task was to bring Russia out of its diplomatic isolation, thus making more unlikely what they (largely incorrectly) were convinced was the continual and major threat to the Soviet state—a renewal of the foreign, and particularly of the British, interventions. They did this during the interwar period, first by improving their relations with the other isolated and weakened power (Germany), and then by trying to find allies in the West against the Nazis (known as Stalin's Popular Front policy).

Neither policy was successful, primarily because of their ideological character. The Soviet rapprochement with Weimar Germany was based on a shared anti-Polish policy, but limited by ideological differences. When Hitler began to rise, Stalin forced the German Communists to fight the Social Democrats rather than the Nazis. Had he been following a policy of Russian national interest only, he would have allied with the Social Democrats and later with the West; and if he had, Hitler's triumphs might have been averted. (True, Britain and France and many Americans preferred Hitler to Stalin, or at least wanted the two to destroy each other; but this was again primarily a reflection of the Communist, rather than the Russian, aspects of Soviet policy. These West Europeans also got the worst of both worlds: by defeating Hitler they so weakened themselves that they lost their primacy in World affairs, *inter alia* because in 1945 not they, but Russia, got control of Eastern and much of Central Europe.)

Nor was Soviet policy in the Far East much more successful—again, in part because of its ideological bent and Stalin's blunders. Although Lenin had initially abandoned all the Tsarist special privileges in China, the weakness of that country made Soviet intervention almost inevitable, if only to prevent Japan from taking advantage of the power vacuum that Republican China presented. Soviet influence became predominant in Outer Mongolia and largely so in Sinkiang, and Moscow kept control over the Chinese Eastern Railway in Manchuria.

In the early and mid-1920s Stalin tried to go further, and blundered badly in the process. The young nationalist Kuomintang movement, under Sun Yat-sen, was attracted to the Soviets, in part because of Lenin's renunciations of Tsarist privileges, and also because the new Soviet system seemed to provide a pattern for Chinese political and economic development and independence from foreign influence. Conversely, Lenin and Stalin, blocked in Western Europe, turned toward Asia, convinced that Moscow should aid anti-colonial regimes in Asia and elsewhere, even if they were non-Communist, in order to combat Western imperialist influence and to prepare the way eventually for Communist revolutions. This was enhanced by Stalin's fear of the British, then .the most powerful foreign power in China. He forced the infant Chinese Communist party to merge into the Kuomintang and to cooperate with it even when, after Sun's death, successor Chiang Kai-shek was preparing to eliminate the Communists.

Stalin was the more obstinate in this course because it had become an issue with his great opponent Trotsky; in this as in many other respects the internal power struggle in Moscow frequently took primacy over Russian national interests. Stalin's policy failed when Chiang crushed the Chinese Communist rising in 1927. Soviet influence in China was thus practically ended until 1945. By the 1930 s Chiang was consolidating his power. The nearly wrecked Chinese Communists revived in Hunan and thereafter—fleeing from Chiang —in Yenan, under the leadership of Mao Tse-tung, who, unlike his predecessors as heads of the Chinese Communist party, was not a Soviet puppet and was probably then already inclined to distrust Moscow's advice.

But by the middle 1930s, from the Soviet perspective any opportunities for Russian gains in China were overshadowed by the danger to Moscow of expanding Japanese imperialism. Slowly and reluctantly Stalin surrendered to Japan the Chinese Eastern Railway in Manchuria. In the hope of stemming Tokyo's expansionism, he moved closer to Chiang Kai-shek. The rise of Japan also began to forge a common interest between the Soviet Union and the United

States. We must, therefore, return to Russo-American relations.

AMERICAN ATTITUDES

American foreign policy in the interwar period was basically isolationist. Public opinion in the United States against the failure of the Wilsonian experiment in international comity led to such an isolationist reaction that those American officials who wanted to carry on an active foreign policy were unable to do so. Moreover, just as in the nineteenth century, there really seemed to be no compelling reasons for such a policy. "The business of the United States," as President Coolidge remarked, "is business." Indeed, American commercial expansion abroad proceeded apace—until the 1929 depression.

Ideological conflict transformed American disinterest in Russia into hostility to Moscow. Native American radicalism had been largely decimated by World War I, and its postwar persecution had been in part stimulated by the associations of part of it with bolshevism. The activities of the Comintern under Lenin and Stalin, the increasing subordination of foreign Communist parties—including the American one—to Moscow, and the opposition of the Bolsheviks not only to traditional American liberal institutions but also to American commercial interests at home and abroad, plus the refusal of the Soviet government to recognize United States claims and debts in Tsarist Russia, and, finally, the domination of conservative Republican administrations in Washington, all combined to make American foreign policy until 1933 hostile to the Soviet Union. Washington's refusal to establish diplomatic relations with the Soviet regime symbolized this hostility. Soviet-American relations did not exist in any real sense until 1933, although American business firms gave considerable technical assistance, in return for financial reward, to Soviet economic development, and American food relief after World War I had saved millions of Russians from starvation. Nor did

Moscow show any great enthusiasm for the improvement of relations with Washington: for the Bolsheviks, the United States was second only to Great Britain in capitalist hostility to Communist aims.

But as in 1905 and 1914 mutual enemies proved more powerful than ideological differences: the revival of German and Japanese expansionism provided the basis for improving Soviet-American relations. American isolationism had never been so complete toward Asia (or toward Latin America) as it had toward Europe, if only because the U.S. Navy and Marines were less unpopular, since less costly in blood, as a means of asserting American influence there. Europe, however, was an area from which many Americans had fled. It seemed under the friendly dominance of the British and the French, and in any case had proved ungrateful for the American blood spent during 1917-18 in its quarrels. When, therefore, in 1931 Japanese expansionism began in Manchuria and, even more, when in 1935 it spilled over into North China, the American government was concerned about bringing a stop to it, albeit without direct American intervention. Its attitude toward the revival of German power under Hitler was similar.

So, indeed, was the Soviet attitude toward both. Stalin, whose foreign policy had always emphasized divisions among his opponents as a means to avoid direct Soviet involvement in war while furthering Soviet aims, was most concerned to persuade other nations to oppose Germany and Japan, or, at least, not to ally with Germany or Japan against him.

In 1933 Stalin was willing to reciprocate Roosevelt's desire to renew diplomatic relations. Both were concerned about Japanese expansionism. Roosevelt did not suffer as much as his predecessors from ideological aversion to bolshevism. But his hopes that relations with Moscow would stop Soviet support of communism in the United States and lead to settlement of the American claims against the Soviet Union proved baseless. Continued mistrust and mutual unwillingness to en-

gage military power against the threats from Tokyo and, increasingly, from Berlin combined to make Soviet-American
relations until 1941 distant and "correct" rather than close.

It required, as it had in 1914-17, the coming of a world
war and a mutual sense of overriding danger from their opponents to bring about anything even close to genuine rapprochement between Moscow and Washington. Initially,
American distrust was intensified greatly by the Soviet-Nazi
Pact in 1939, and even more by the Soviet invasion of Finland. Only the persistence of isolationism prevented the development in Washington of a sentiment similar to that in
London and Paris for intervention against the Soviets. Even
the Nazi invasion of Russia in mid-1941 was not sufficient to
bring about a drastic shift in U.S. public opinion in the
Soviets' favor. (The day after the invasion, the then Senator
Harry S Truman declared in the Senate that the United States
should aid Russia when Germany was winning and aid Germany when Russia was winning, toward the aim of having
both destroy each other!) But the Japanese attack on Pearl
Harbor on December 7, 1941 and the subsequent entry of
Germany into the war against the United States changed all
this and brought about a new, if only apparent, honeymoon
in Soviet-American relations.

2

The United States and China in Modern History

Until the late 1930s the primary interest of the United States in China was commercial rather than political or military. Moreover, not the United States, but Britain, Russia, and Japan were the major powers concerned with Chinese affairs. The United States tended to follow their lead for two reasons: first, Washington and the American people were still fundamentally isolationist—they had no intention of becoming involved in "entangling alliances" in Europe, and still less in Asia; and second, the United States conveniently and effortlessly profited economically from the encroachments of these powers in Imperial China.

By the beginning of the nineteenth century, when the newly independent United States began to have some commercial contacts with China, the Manchu Empire in Peking was in an advanced stage of decline. Its mandarins were increasingly corrupt, its emperors less able, and its culture stagnant, as compared with the height of the dynasty. Yet, this alone would not have disrupted China; it was fundamentally the impact of the West which brought that about. For thousands of years China had considered itself—usually with very considerable reason—to be the center of human culture and civilization. For the Chinese elite, all other peoples were "foreign barbarians" whom the emperor graciously allowed to bring tribute to the Chinese throne, but who were in no sense equal to the Chinese "Middle Kingdom." Moreover, China was for most of its history the predominant power in East and Southeast Asia—in Korea, Indochina, Thailand, and Burma, whose rulers had normally acknowledged Chinese suzerainty. The Chinese Empire was accustomed to symbolizing its disdain of the "foreign barbarians" by refusing them any access to its country, and, above all, to its capital in Peking.

FOREIGN POWERS IN CHINA

Foreign contacts with China had in fact begun long before the United States became independent. In the seventeenth century Italian Jesuits had played an important role at the Imperial Court in Peking. In the late seventeenth century Russian Cossacks, plunging east from the Grand Duchy of Muscovy, had reached the Pacific Ocean and encountered the boundaries of the Chinese Empire, which then included what is now the Soviet Maritime Province as well as the present eastern part of Soviet Central Asia. The immediate result of this first Russo-Chinese encounter, the Treaty of Nerchinsk in 1689, was a standoff, plus the establishment of a small Russian trading mission in Peking. The Portuguese also established a trading post at Macao, and by the late eighteenth century the British, already firmly established in India, also began to trade, under rather humiliating conditions, with the major southern Chinese port of Canton. They, like other merchants there, were confined to a narrow area and forced to deal only through certain Chinese merchants, without any access to the

Imperial Viceroy of the city and without, of course, any diplomatic relations with the Imperial Court in Peking.

The British were not willing indefinitely to accept the Chinese refusal to deal with foreigners on the basis of equality, and in 1840-41 an Anglo-Chinese war, arising out of the profitable British opium trade, forced Peking to abandon its haughty isolation, to increase trade privileges to include four other ports, to allow British consuls to reside in these ports, and to cede the island of Hong Kong to Britain. The Americans, who had remained neutral in the war, were quick to profit from it. In the 1844 Treaty of Wanghia, they obtained even more than the British had, notably the privilege of extraterritoriality; namely, that American citizens charged with crimes in China would be tried only by American consuls— without, of course, any equivalent concession with respect to Chinese citizens in the United States.

CHINESE-AMERICAN RELATIONS

Thus was established the pattern of Chinese-American relations until 1930: the United States, after protesting the encroachments by the European powers—and later by Japan as well—upon Chinese sovereignty, would take care to profit equally from them, with the one exception that it would not annex any Chinese territory. This was a quite normal course of policy for its time, and the United States certainly did not take the initiative in the semi-colonial exploitation and dismemberment of China; the British, the Russians, and the Japanese did that. Moreover, the American missionaries who in the mid-nineteenth century began to flood into China did much unselfish work in medicine and education. Yet, they often demanded, and got, United States protection against Chinese interference with them. Furthermore, during this period there were always two tendencies in American policy: those liberals in Washington and elsewere who favored American support of the sovereignty and territorial integrity of China, and those others, usually commercial and later imperialist elements, supported by the American merchants in the China trade, who wanted the United States to profit as much as possible from China's weakness.

During the nineteenth century, as Western encroachment in China continued and the impotence of the Manchu rulers to prevent it became increasingly obvious, anti-Western sentiment among the Chinese developed rapidly. Its first outbreak was the Taiping rebellion, in the middle of the century. Many Americans, like other Westerners in China, felt that any other regime would be preferable to the Manchus and therefore favored the rebellion, but Washington decided that its success would probably lead to anarchy and the subsequent division of China between Britain and Russia, thus threatening American interests. Washington, therefore, clearly foreshadowing Secretary of State John Hay's famous Open Door policy at the turn of the century, favored the Imperial government in Peking. Thus, the Americans could congratulate themselves on noninterference and the support of the legitimate Chinese government, while many increasingly nationalist Chinese saw in the American position only a hypocritical trick designed to preserve American commercial privileges, if not increase them, vis-à-vis Chinese resistance and the threat of British or Russian monopolization of them.

This scenario recurred several times. In the late 1850s the British and French occupied Peking in order to force the emperor to receive their envoys and to grant them more privileges; and again the Americans stood by and profited from the result. But other American forces were also at work: for example, Anson Burlingame, the United States envoy in Peking from 1861 to 1868, worked so hard to protect Chinese as well as American interests that upon his retirement the emperor designated him as the head of a Chinese mission to tour the United States and Europe. His efforts, however, were in the end frustrated by the continued refusal of Peking, and in particular of the dowager empress Tsu Hsi, who for all practical purposes ruled China during the later nineteenth century, to abandon the traditional Chinese policy of isolation.

During the late nineteenth century Chinese-American relations were much worsened, and anti-American sentiment among the younger educated Chinese greatly increased, by the American insistence upon ending the immigration of Chinese coolies into the United States. They had been brought there because of the great labor shortage, but their industriousness and low standard of living soon gave rise, notably in California, to strong economic and racial hostility toward them. For all practical purposes, Chinese immigration, in spite of initial American pledges to the contrary, was halted until 1943, and Chinese-American relations deeply poisoned as a result.

Until the end of the nineteenth century, American relations with China had reflected unrealized American expectations of profits from the China trade. In 1898, with the Spanish-American War and the American annexation of the Philippines, American imperialism of a more political nature entered the scene, and Washington became increasingly determined to become a Pacific power. Indeed, in retrospect the annexation of the Philippines, and the resultant necessity, as Washington saw it, for naval forces and bases to protect the islands, catapulted the United States into the politics of East and Southeast Asia—a position from which the United States has never escaped.

It was within this context, as well as that of British fears that Russia would dominate China, that Secretary of State John Hay in 1900 propagated the Open Door policy. Initially, this amounted only to a mutual recognition of spheres of influence; that is, of the status quo, by the United States and the other foreign powers in China. In that same year, however, this policy was challenged by the second great outbreak in modern Chinese history of anti-foreign sentiment—the Boxer Rebellion. The United States sent a military force to participate in the relief of the Legation Quarter in Peking, where the foreign diplomats were for some months menaced with massacre by the Boxers, half-heartedly supported by the Dowager Empress. In order to try to prevent the other powers from taking the opportunity to dismember China still further, Hay unilaterally expanded the Open Door policy in July 1900 to include the support of independence and territorial integrity of China.

Thereafter, the main threats to Chinese independence and territories came from Russia and Japan. Initially, fearing Russian encroachments in Manchuria, Washington favored Japan in the 1905 Russo-Japanese war, but the Japanese victory and Tokyo's subsequent acquisition of Russian positions in Manchuria awakened the United States to what was to remain the predominant concern of American policy for the next forty years: to prevent Japan from dismembering and dominating China—without, however, until the late 1930s bringing anything much more than political and moral pressures to bear on Tokyo. The 1911 collapse of the Manchu dynasty and the resultant greater weakness of China increased American fear of Japanese predominance in China. There were some rather meaningless American-Japanese compromises, such as the 1917 Lansing-Ishii agreement reaffirming both Chinese territorial integrity and simultaneously affirming Japanese "special interests" in China, and Japan's partial acquisition of former German interests in China in the 1919 Treaty of Versailles, when Wilson accepted what he considered an unsatisfactory compromise and thus deeply offended both Japan and China. Moreover, the American military force sent after World War I to Vladivostok, while ostensibly directed against the Bolsheviks, was at least as much intended to prevent Japan from getting control over Eastern Siberia. In the 1921 Nine-Power Treaty, Washington did succeed in getting Japan to pledge respect for China's independence and territorial integrity.

Meanwhile, in China the Nationalist government was by the mid-1920 s gradually beginning to expand its authority.

Pushed forward by the wave of nationalism which had gripped young, westernized Chinese intellectuals and reflecting their determination to recover China's independence and to remove foreign influence over it, the new government pressed the foreign powers to give up their concessions obtained by the "unequal treaties," in particular, extraterritoriality. This put the United States in an uncomfortable position, forced to choose between its professed principles and its commercial interests. In spite of pressure from the latter, Washington moved faster than did the other powers in surrendering its special tariff and extraterritoriality privileges, thus improving Chinese-American relations.

Communism in China

The advent to power of the Bolsheviks in Russia in 1917 had led to a major change in Russo-Chinese relations. Lenin surrendered all Russian special privileges in China, with the exception of Russian interests in the Chinese Eastern Railway in Manchuria. Moreover, in the early 1920s the Bolsheviks established close ties with Sun Yat-sen and his Nationalist government, sending him advisers and supporting him in his campaign against Western special privileges. But Moscow also was deeply involved with the formation and expansion of the Chinese Communist party and was responsible for its infiltration of and merging with the Nationalist Kuomintang, in the hope, so Stalin and the Chinese Communists calculated, of eventually controlling it.

However, Stalin, absorbed in his struggle with Trotsky for Lenin's succession, unwisely pushed the Chinese Communists, menaced by Chiang Kai-shek, into risings in Canton and Shanghai against the will of their leaders. Chiang, by then Sun Yat-sen's obvious successor, crushed the risings; the Chinese Communist leadership fled to Moscow and to the rural areas, where the young Mao Tse-tung by 1935 took over the party leadership; and Soviet influence in China declined greatly. By the mid-1930s Moscow felt itself as much menaced as Washington by the rise of Japanese imperialism, the more so since Hitler's coming to power in Germany in 1933 more immediately menaced the Soviet Union than it did the United States. Stalin thus became increasingly favorable to Chiang Kai-shek and, therefore, less concerned to support the Chinese Communists against him.

THE THREAT OF JAPAN

All these new tendencies became clear after the Japanese resumed their expansion, invading Manchuria in 1931 and North China in 1937. Under the leadership of Secretary of State Henry Stimson, Washington in 1931 went far in verbal condemnation of the Japanese action, even to the point of expressing American willingness in principle to cooperate with the League of Nations against it. But Britain and France were no more willing to take effective action against Japan in 1931 and thereafter than they were against Hitler, so nothing was done. (It is doubtful that the United States would have used force in any case.)

At first, as the Sino-Japanese struggle increased and Hitler's victories in Europe made another world war seem more likely, American public reaction was a reversion to isolation. However, as Japanese expansion and brutality in China continued, by the late 1930s American public opinion began to favor pressure against Japan. In neither of these cases, however, did the American conception of its interests in China itself play a decisive role. American hostility to Japan intensified from a combination of emotional revulsion, desire to protect commercial interests, and, above all, the desire to prevent East Asia from falling under the influence of one hostile imperialist power—one, moreover, allied with equally hostile Nazi Germany, itself threatening to dominate Europe.

Once Hitler had conquered France and the Netherlands, Japan intensified its efforts to acquire control over Indochina and the Dutch East Indies (Indonesia). Washington, confronted with its worst fears come true—Great Britain and China both gravely menaced and Japan and Germany allied—immediately intensified its military and economic aid to China and announced its intention to surrender all its special privileges in China. (Chiang Kai-shek had been by this time driven back into the interior, with his capital at Chungking, and the Japanese dominated the China coast.) Only Washington's desire to prevent war with Japan while the United States was still unprepared, plus the priority it gave to Europe, made it slowly increase its economic pressure on Japan. Even so, a Japanese-American clash was only a question of time: the United States was not prepared to accept exclusive Japanese domination of East and Southeast Asia, and Japan would settle for nothing less.

When the United States cut off all trade, including oil, with Japan in mid-1941, thus in effect declaring economic war, Tokyo decided to fight. The result was the Japanese attack on Pearl Harbor on December 7, 1941, and the subsequent entry of the United States into the war, not only against Japan but against Germany, which declared war on the United States as well.

3

United States–Russian Relations During World War II

Neither Russia nor the United States wanted World War II. Both emerged from it, after the collapse of Germany and Japan and of Western Europe and China as well, as the only superpowers in the world. Hitler, who far more than anyone else began it, was dominated not only by violent pan-German chauvinism but also by malignant neo-Darwinist expansionism, which centered on the physical liquidation of the Jews, the conquest of the Soviet Union and the enslavement of the Slavs, and the eventual domination of the world. He came as close as he did to this aim because of his own—however evil—genius, of the energies he tapped and drove forward in the German people, of the blunders and short-sightedness of the British and the French, plus the inaction of the Americans, and, not least, of Stalin's errors. Stalin forced the German Communists to concentrate their struggle against the Social Democrats and not the Nazis, thus helping Hitler

28

to come to power, and, more importantly, he signed a pact with Hitler in 1939 whereby Berlin and Moscow divided Poland. The German leader, with his eastern flank at least temporarily secure, could then safely destroy France.

Stalin hoped, by the Soviet-Nazi Pact, to postpone or, if not completely, then to deflect a Nazi assault on Russia; and many in Britain and France hoped—in vain—that they could deflect Hitler against Russia instead of themselves. Stalin probably had two other aims: first, to embroil the capitalist powers with each other and thereby strengthen Russia and communism, and, second, to gain territory to the west—the Baltic States, Eastern Poland, Northern Bukovina, and Bessarabia, which the British and French would not have given him. These territories had, except for Bukovina, belonged to the Tsars, and, like Stalin's successful demand at Yalta for Port Arthur and Dairen, one could view their return to the Soviet Union simply as the restoration of lost Russian territory, necessary for protection against any repetition of Japanese and German aggression—in short, an essentially moderate move compatible with Russian defensive national interests as opposed to imperialist expansionism. But Stalin's true aims went much further, as was revealed not only by his postwar hegemony over Eastern Europe but before, by Molotov's demands on Ribbentrop in late 1940, when the two were negotiating the future of Europe: hegemony over Yugoslavia, Hungary, Greece, and Western Poland as well as control over the Danish and Turkish straits and the mouth of the Danube. Not surprisingly, Hitler considered them unacceptable and thereafter he renewed his decision, first taken in July 1940, to attack Russia before England was defeated.

The Nazi attack began in June 1941, and although it reached the gates of Moscow and later the Caucasus, Russia survived, primarily by dint of its own efforts but also as a result of massive Western, primarily American, aid.

ROOSEVELT'S POLICIES

Even before the Nazi attack on the Soviet Union, Churchill had decided that he would give maximum aid to Stalin in order to attain Britain's essential aim—Hitler's defeat. Roosevelt was disposed to do the same; and throughout the war American lend-lease aid was given to the Russians in massive quantities without any political conditions, even though Churchill—once it was clear that Hitler was defeated —attempted in 1943 and thereafter to revise Western strategy to include the containment of postwar Russian expansion as well as the defeat of Germany. There has been much criticism since about this, and many have maintained that Roosevelt did not do all that he could have to limit Russian expansionism. It is therefore worthwhile to outline briefly what really happened.

First, Roosevelt and Churchill were afraid that if they did not support Russia completely, Stalin would make a separate peace with Hitler and not enter the war against Japan. There were some Nazi-Soviet peace feelers, but they came to nothing, primarily because of Hitler's refusal to make any concessions. In any case, it seems unlikely that Stalin would have made peace. Second, while Churchill was quite aware of the dangers of Russian predominance in postwar Europe, Roosevelt seems to have viewed the postwar world as one in which the Soviet Union would inevitably be the strongest power in Europe but one in which, as Cordell Hull once put it, spheres of influence would disappear and the United Nations would embody a worldwide security system—surely an illusion, in view of Stalin's previous and subsequent policies. Roosevelt also thought that if the United Nations did not work satisfactorily, Britain and Russia could take care of Europe while the United States would concentrate on the Pacific. Third, Roosevelt—and Churchill as well—had to cope with the enflamed, simplicist wartime emotions of the American and

British peoples, for most of whom "Good Old Uncle Joe" was a brave ally, not a potential enemy. Fourth, to Roosevelt and Churchill the total evil of the Hitler regime required its complete defeat and unconditional surrender, even at the cost of a major increase of Russian influence. Fifth, Roosevelt assumed that the American people would not be prepared to keep forces in Europe long after the war.

Yet, all this having been said, Roosevelt and the American government were, it seems, in part responsible for Soviet expansion into Central and Eastern Europe. FDR was, of course, no Communist or "fellow traveler"; but like most successful politicians, he was a vain man, and he was supremely confident that he could "handle" Stalin. Yet, Stalin was, as George F. Kennan has written:

> . . . a fantastically cruel and crafty political personality, viewing with deadly enmity everything, whether within Russia or outside it, which did not submit abjectly to his own authority; a personality the suspiciousness of which assumed forms positively pathological; a personality informed by the most profound cynicism and contempt for human nature, dominated by an insatiable ambition, driven by a burning envy for all qualities it did not itself possess, intolerant of every sort of rival, or even independent, authority or influence. . . .

Roosevelt, on the other hand, in addition to his vanity, was strongly and emotionally anti-German, having as a schoolboy in Germany, as he said in 1945, "formed an early distaste for German arrogance and provincialism." Moreover, contrary to Churchill, he was ideologically as well as emotionally involved in the war, as had been Wilson in 1917, and thus less amenable to arguments about the balance of power.

This contributed greatly to his refusal to have any dealings with the German anti-Nazi resistance. The latter's peace aims as late as 1943 were still so imbued with German predominance in Europe that it is doubtful if any such dealings could have been successful, even though, in retrospect, one of the few ways to have kept the Russians out of Central Europe would have been to have made peace, if necessary without the Soviets, with an anti-Nazi and anti-Communist German resistance. But American and British public opinion would have been strongly opposed to it, and neither Roosevelt nor Churchill ever considered it. In any case, the failure of the July 20, 1944, attempt to overthrow Hitler ended this possibility.

Moreover, Roosevelt was strongly anti-colonialist and thus tended to identify France and Great Britain with what he considered rightly doomed colonial empires. And, finally, Roosevelt, his generals, and, indeed, most Americans (State Department experts on Russia like Kennan were notable exceptions) concentrated on winning the war; what happened thereafter was to them much less important. They disregarded —to America's subsequent disadvantage—the reverse of Clausewitz's dictum: with Stalin peace would be the continuation of war by other means. Stalin, who did not disregard it, profited thereby.

In short, then, although Roosevelt's support of Great Britain in 1940, against the advice of almost all his advisers, contributed greatly to its survival and Hitler's defeat, and, with his successful fight against the depression, made him one of the great American Presidents, the record of his dealings with Stalin reflects illusion, shortsightedness, and, in retrospect, failure to achieve his aim—United States security through a continuation of the wartime anti-Hitler coalition.

The failure of Roosevelt's policy of conciliation toward Stalin first became apparent with respect to Poland. Britain had gone to war over Poland, and the United States was sympathetic to the Polish cause. Stalin had annexed Eastern Poland in 1939 and was determined to keep it. He had broken off relations with the London Polish government-in-exile during the war over their demand for an investigation of the murder of thousands of Polish officers at Katyn—a murder for which, most scholars are now agreed, the Soviets were themselves responsible—and had set up a puppet Polish Communist Lublin committee instead. He had held his army on the opposite bank of the Vistula in 1944 while the Nazis crushed the Warsaw rising. (The political goal of the rising was to have a free, non-Communist Polish government established in Warsaw when the Red Army arrived; this Stalin was, understandably, determined to prevent.) That would have been the last time for Washington and London, by threatening and if necessary going through with a cut off of aid to the Soviets, to try with some hope of success to keep Poland out of Stalin's hands; but Roosevelt was not prepared to do so. As the Red Army entered Poland, the Soviets arrested the non-Communist Polish underground leaders and rapidly imposed increasingly monolithic Communist rule on the country.

The Yalta conference in early 1945 centered on the Polish question. (It also produced a Soviet commitment to enter the war against Japan, for which Roosevelt was willing to make concessions—unnecessary, as it turned out, since the Japanese were beaten anyway.) Stalin made some formal concessions to the Western insistence on "free elections" in Poland, but in fact it was too late at Yalta to do anything about Poland, for the Red Army had already occupied it. As Kennan, then minister-counsellor in the United States Embassy in Moscow, wrote in his diary on August 1, 1944, when the Polish exile prime minister Mikołajczyk was in Moscow vainly negotiating with Stalin for Poland's freedom and the Nazis were crushing the Warsaw rising while the Red Army stood idly by:

> Russian conceptions of tolerance would not go far beyond those things with which Russians were themselves familiar; . . . the Russian police system would inevitably seep into Polish life unless sharp measures were taken on the Polish side to counteract it, and . . . such countermeasures would inevitably be deemed provocative and anti-Russian in Moscow. I knew, in short, that there is no border zone of Russian power. The

jealous and intolerant eye of the Kremlin can distinguish, in the end, only vassals and enemies; and the neighbors of Russia, if they do not wish to be the one, must reconcile themselves to being the other. In the face of this knowledge, I could only feel that there was something frivolous about our whole action in this Polish question. I reflected on the light-heartedness with which great powers offer advice to smaller ones in matters affecting the vital interests of the latter. I was sorry to find myself, for the moment, a part of this. And I wished that instead of mumbling words of official optimism we had had the judgment and the good taste to bow our heads in silence before the tragedy of a people who have been our allies, whom we have helped to save from our enemies, and whom we cannot save from our friends.[1]

Much the same happened with Bulgaria, Rumania, and Hungary, with no effective Western opposition. Czechoslovakia remained at least formally a democracy until early 1948, when the Communists took over; but the Czechoslovak Communists had control of the key positions in the Prague government in 1945. The February 1948 coup made total and public what had in large part been the case before. Tito's Yugoslavia, which until 1948 also controlled Albania, was until then pro-Soviet, but not under total Soviet domination, as 1948 showed.

POSTWAR CONFLICTS

The second great issue between the United States and Russia after World War II was Germany; and it remains to this day the most irreconcilable subject of conflict between them. During the war the Americans, British, and Russians seemed agreed that Germany should be occupied, partitioned, kept at a minimal standard of living, and deprived of much of its eastern territory. Stalin, as the Americans and British gradually realized, intended to deprive Germany of very

[1] George F. Kennan, *Memoirs 1925-1950* (Boston: Little Brown, 1967), pp. 209-210.

much territory indeed. He wanted everything east of the Oder and the Western Neisse, including all of Pomerania, Silesia, and East Prussia, to be given to Poland as compensation for its lost eastern territories and—in fact—in order to bind it permanently, on an anti-German basis, to Soviet policy, as well as to make sure that Moscow would have a card in reserve vis-à-vis a future Germany. (A correct calculation—and one of Stalin's most cynically brilliant strokes of diplomacy.)

During the war the Americans, British, and Russians agreed upon a division of postwar Germany into zones of occupation, with Berlin, in the center of the Soviet zone, also divided into four sectors. Unfortunately, in spite of warnings by some American diplomats, Washington did not insist on a firm guarantee of a corridor to the city.

All the occupying powers had committed themselves to the "four D's"; de-Nazification, demilitarization, deindustrialization, and democratization. Stalin understood these terms, of course, differently from his wartime allies. His postwar aims in Germany were simple: keep Germany weak; get German labor and reparations to rebuild the Soviet Union; and, by a Soviet veto over its administration, prevent Germany from ever again menacing Russia either by itself or as an ally of other imperialist powers.

Indeed, there is little if any reason to believe that Stalin *ever* envisaged the continuation of the wartime alliance. He regarded the Western capitalist states as his inveterate enemies; he anticipated a worldwide struggle with the United States; and he was determined to reverse the wartime domestic liberalization he had accorded the Soviet people—something which would be inhibited by a continuation of good relations with the West and furthered by antagonism with it.

Moreover, one new, revolutionary, and decisive factor had transformed world politics—nuclear weapons. Obtained first by the Americans, with British assistance, they made the United States temporarily *the* superpower, since no state, including the Soviet Union, could destroy the atom-armed United States, and the United States could destroy any state in the world. From the beginning Stalin was determined to give absolute and total priority toward obtaining atomic weapons for Russia, no matter what the cost—another reason for repression and armament rather than consumer-goods expenditures at home. Simultaneously, the American atomic capability made Stalin even more cautious than he had always been with respect to a risk of war, particularly with the United States. Finally, of course, it made him all the more determined to hold Germany down and prevent it from ever again becoming industrially powerful, and therefore capable of achieving atomic capacity.

Truman's Policies

Germany was not the only area where postwar United States-Russian conflicts developed; indeed, the first clashes came elsewhere. Moreover, they came with a new American President—Harry S Truman. Although one cannot be sure how Roosevelt would have reacted to postwar events, it seems probable, in view of some of his statements just before he died in April 1945, that he would have turned against Stalin as well. In any case, Truman was less ideological, less idealistic, less vain, certainly less gifted, but perhaps even more determined than Roosevelt. His background and political inclinations gradually brought somewhat more conservative and more anti-Soviet officials into power in Washington. Stalin's refusal, in Truman's view, to carry out his commitments made at Yalta with respect to democratization in Poland led to a clash between Truman and Molotov, which although without results for Poland disillusioned Truman rapidly about Soviet aims and policies.

Soviet reluctance to evacuate their troops from northern Iran (Azerbaijan) in 1946 led to something close to an ultimatum from Truman, which contributed to the troops being withdrawn. At the end of the war the British had forcibly suppressed a Communist-led attempt to take power in Greece, while Stalin, faithful to his agreement with Churchill putting Greece into the British sphere of influence, stood by without protest. Thereafter, the Greek Communists began a civil war in which, as we now know but did not then, they were primarily supported by the then extremist Yugoslav Communists, with Stalin counseling caution rather than urging them on.

By 1947 the British, in the first major sign of their postwar exhaustion, declared themselves unable to further carry the burden of aid to Greece and Turkey, and Truman took it over—thus making clear that the United States was determined, as the British had been, to keep the Soviets out of the Mediterranean, and, indeed, in the universality of the Truman Doctrine's rhetoric, to contain them throughout the world.

Moreover, by 1947 the United States realized with increasing apprehension, as Stalin must have with pleasure, the extent and seriousness of the collapse of the power of Western Europe. Britain, France, the Low Countries, and Italy were all exhausted by the war—spiritually, politically, and, above all, economically. Their industries, particularly in Great Britain, were not pulling out of the slump; in France and Italy large Communist parties were in the government; and the desolateness of West Germany, before the war one of the industrial centers of the world, contributed still more to the crisis. It became clear to Truman and his advisers that economic recovery and political stability, and with it the balance of power in Europe, were now threatened even more by the vacuum in the West of the continent than by the expansionist power to the east, and could only be restored if (a) massive American aid were poured in and (b) the industrial potential of western Germany were utilized to aid in the recovery of Western Europe—thereby preventing West

Germany, and the continent as a whole, either coming under Soviet control or remaining permanently a burden on the American taxpayer.

Confrontation in Europe

The stage was thus set for the major Soviet-American postwar confrontation, over Germany and Europe. There was, we can now see in retrospect, something existential, structural, indeed, almost inevitable about the conflict. Postwar Western Europe was a political vacuum, something which politics, like nature, abhors; and if it were not restored to economic and political health its Communist parties would likely take it over. And even if Russia never intended to occupy and control Western Europe (we may remember that Stalin said one reason France was not Communist was that the Red Army had not been able to get that far), could Stalin have been reasonably expected to resist a call for aid from Thorez and Togliatti, his French and Italian Communist allies, if he need not have feared American opposition?

Conversely, for Stalin, his postwar European policy gave priority to two minimum objectives, control over Eastern Europe and keeping Germany down. But if the West were to revive West Germany, the second would become impossible and in the long run the first would be endangered. His opposition to the American insistence upon West German recovery was therefore both predictable and, from his viewpoint, inevitable and justified.

On the other hand, were the West—and that meant the United States—determined to fill the European power vacuum, as Truman and his advisers came to be, lest Moscow fill it instead, this meant the economic and therefore the political revival of West Germany. But such a West German revival inevitably meant turning the balance of power again against the Soviet Union, since it could hope for no equivalent in the smaller and weaker East Germany, out of which Stalin was determined to drag reparations and thus inevitably keep weak.

Although some Americans, such as George Kennan, were convinced from the beginning that there was no alternative to the reconstruction of West Germany as a part of the reconstruction of Western Europe, in order first to contain and eventually to help diminish Soviet power in the middle of Europe, it took two years after the end of the war until Truman and his advisers came to the same conclusion.

After the Russians rejected Secretary of State Byrnes' proposal for a united neutralized Germany and proceeded rapidly to sovietize their zone—East Germany—and after Stalin also began to enforce increasing conformity and sovietization on his East European satellites, the United States proceeded rapidly with the economic reconstruction of Western Europe, including West Germany. Its main instrument for this was the Marshall Plan of massive, centrally administered economic aid, perhaps the greatest success of postwar United States foreign policy. This inevitably involved the economic and then the political unity of the three western German zones and the introduction of a new currency for them in order to overcome the inflation rampant in postwar Germany.

The Berlin Blockade

The introduction of this new currency in the western sectors of Berlin was taken by the Soviets as the occasion for the Berlin Blockade, which for more than a year (1948-49) isolated the western sectors of the city and which was abandoned by Stalin only after the United States demonstrated, by the introduction of the Berlin airlift under the leadership of General Lucius Clay, that it could and would indefinitely supply the city from the air. In 1949, then, Stalin gave up this first attempt to maintain, if not to expand, his position in Germany.

Was the Berlin Blockade an effort to expand or only to maintain the Russian position in Germany and in Europe? It is an important question. The Blockade was an attempt to maintain the Soviet position against the Western decision to unite and economically reconstruct their zones, along with the rest of Western Europe, which would and did inevitably shift the balance of power in the Western favor. Conversely, the rapid sovietization of the Russian zone, to which Stalin and Walter Ulbricht seemed committed, would cut or at least greatly diminish the ability of West Germany to influence East Germany, if only by the attraction of its economic recovery; and this a Soviet takeover of West Berlin would have done. Finally, although this was not fully realized in the West at the time, the Soviet position in Eastern Europe was already menaced by the approaching expulsion of Yugoslavia from the "socialist camp."

Marshal Tito, although in the 1930s a faithful servant of Stalin, had come to power in Yugoslavia by winning a partisan war, with much Western but little Russian support, against the German occupiers of his country. After 1945 his domestic policies were super-Stalinist and his international policy was even more anti-American than Moscow's. But, infused with the pride of a successful partisan struggle, he was determined not only to run Yugoslavia but also to form and lead a Balkan federation, including Albania, Bulgaria, and part of northern Greece; and, as we now know, he, more than Stalin, supported and urged on the Greek Communists in their civil war.

None of this Stalin was willing to accept. On the contrary, he was determined to infiltrate and control the Yugoslav Communist party, army, and security police, just as he did elsewhere in Eastern Europe. Moreover, he and his then principal associate Andrei Zhdanov seem to have decided in 1945 and thereafter to adopt a more forward policy, not only in the West but also throughout the "third world." In 1948 there were, for example, a series of attempted guerrilla risings in India and Southeast Asia in which Moscow probably played a part. Finally, Stalin was determined to crack down on liberalization and deviation at home and reverse the effect of his wartime internal concessions. In part, probably, as a consequence of this general turn toward extremism, but also, almost surely, as a result of the revival in him of his pathological suspicion of all divergencies from his own will which had characterized his great purges in the mid-1930s, Stalin set out to force complete conformity and complete Soviet control at all levels of authority in Eastern Europe.

When Tito proved unwilling to bend to Stalin's will in this respect, Stalin in 1947 began to try to force Tito to capitulate to Soviet hegemony. After Tito's refusal, Stalin in mid-1948 read him out of the socialist camp, soon thereafter denounced him as an "American imperialist agent," and began a witchhunt throughout Eastern Europe for his real or, more often, alleged supporters. This led to purges in all the East European countries, to the revolt of Albania against Yugoslavia in favor of Soviet hegemony, and in general to the imposition of extreme Stalinism in the area. It had also contributed to the February 1948 Communist take-over in Czechoslovakia. There the Czechoslovak Communists had since the war held all the key positions, but on the surface a coalition with the democratic parties and with President Beneš was maintained. But when in early 1948 the forthcoming elections seemed likely to bring a Communist defeat, and when Stalin turned to extremism throughout the bloc, fearing the rise of a powerful West Germany and the effects of Tito's (still secret) defiance, the non-Communist ministers resigned, and the Czech Communists, aided by full Soviet support and America's and Beneš's inaction, took over complete power.

Thus when in summer 1948 Stalin imposed the Berlin blockade, he was faced with the Yugoslav defection. Was, then, the Berlin blockade, as well as the Prague coup, a defensive measure, to preserve what he had and compensate for the rise of West Germany? In considerable part it prob-

ably was; and its failure may have contributed toward making Stalin's policy in East Germany and in Eastern Europe
even more extreme. But it was inevitably also, whether or
not Stalin intended it to be, expansionist in character. For
if it had succeeded and the United States had given up West
Berlin, the developing stability in West Germany and Western Europe would almost surely have begun to decline, and
new opportunities and a new power vacuum presented to
Stalin, which he probably would not have felt able to resist.
Thus, as has been the case throughout the whole postwar
era, the partition of Germany and of Europe and the Western
enclave in West Berlin were by their nature potentially destabilizing factors, since their transformation in the favor of
either superpower would inevitably result in further, more
far-reaching destabilizing effects.

Nuclear Power and Communist Growth. Two other
very important events occurred in 1949 which had profound
and lasting effects for Soviet-American and Chinese-American
relations, the attainment by the Russians of atomic capacity and
the conquest of power in China by the Chinese Communists.

The former, which was followed in 1953 by the Soviet
achievement of hydrogen bomb capacity, shortly after the
similar American achievement, has until now contributed
greatly to the primacy of the two atomic superpowers, the
United States and the Soviet Union, over all other states, as
well as to the peace of the world. For by greatly increasing
the risk of escalation from conventional to nuclear war and
by replacing the postwar American atomic monoply by a
nuclear stalemate between the two powers, it in effect
froze national boundaries, particularly those of the superpowers themselves as well as those in Europe, where the conventional confrontation was so close and total that any attempt
to change them became, because of the risk of escalation, extremely unlikely. Thus Soviet hopes of expansion into Western
Europe, as well as American hopes of a reversal by outside
influence of the Soviet control over Eastern Europe, were both

disappointed. Not that Soviet and American influence in Europe was to remain static; but it was to change primarily because of European developments within—for example, France and Rumania—rather than by the efforts of Washington or Moscow.

CHINA GOES COMMUNIST

United States containment policy in Europe after 1945 was by and large successful; but in the Far East, although Japan remained under American influence, China exchanged Nationalist for Communist rule and Moscow, not Washington, became—for a time—China's main ally. Why?

Washington understood Europe better than the Far East, felt that its main interests were there, and dealt there with governments and peoples which while weakened by the war were still developed, industrialized areas sharing the same Western culture. In China, on the contrary, the United States faced a vast, underdeveloped country with a government demoralized by eight years of war and confronted with a strong, native Communist movement hardened by decades of armed struggle against the Kuomintang. Washington could not have "saved" either Western Europe or China from Communist control by its own efforts alone; and while Western Europe largely saved itself, the Kuomintang regime was too demoralized to do the same. Washington did not, therefore, "lose" China; Mao conquered the resigned if not willing Chinese.

Imperial Japan has been the great success story of modernization and industrialization in the modern Far East; Chiang's Kuomintang was the great failure. Originally revolutionary, the Kuomintang moved toward bureaucracy, conservatism, and reaction; and in the process, to preserve its own power, it increasingly alienated, first to passivity and then largely to communism, the young, modernizing intellectuals of China. Even so, it is highly doubtful that the Chinese

Communists would have come to power, or at least not so soon and so completely, had it not been for the eight-year Sino-Japanese war. With all its faults, the Kuomintang in 1935 was gradually consolidating its power, and Mao was in the caves of far northwest Yenan. But in eight years the war so demoralized and wrecked China, so destroyed its economy by inflation, gave such opportunities to the Communists, and so confined Chiang to far western Szechuan, that by 1945 the Nationalists could not seize the opportunities they were offered.

These opportunities were not unlimited. First, the Kuomintang armies were themselves weakened by the years of war and by incompetent and corrupt commanders and leadership. Second, the concessions Roosevelt made to Stalin at Yalta, without the participation of China, to get Russia into the Japanese war—based upon an overestimate of Japanese resistance and, therefore, of the necessity of Soviet participation—returned to Russia the ports that she had lost in 1905 in Manchuria. Consequently, when at the end of the war, as had been agreed between the Chinese Nationalists, the Americans, and the Russians, Chiang's armies tried to reoccupy Manchuria from the Japanese, they found the Chinese Communists already in possession. The Soviets had handed the Japanese arms captured there over to them. Finally, although the Americans gave considerable postwar economic aid to Chiang, and transported his troops by air and sea to reoccupy the Japanese-held areas (except Manchuria), neither Washington nor—more importantly—the American people was prepared to commit anything like the financial and military resources they had expended in Western Europe to prevent communism from winning in China.

It still remains doubtful if the United States could have, or in its own interests should have, intervened in China to save Chiang's regime. The collapse of the Nationalists reflected not only military incompetence but also—far more importantly—the conviction of the majority of the Chinese elite that

Chiang's government would not and could not effectively modernize China and restore it to great-power status; that is, achieve the aims of Sun Yat-sen's revolution. Nor did Mao and his associates seem to the Chinese elite, as they (wrongly) did to most Americans, to be agents or satellites of the Russians; rather, the Chinese Communists were viewed as fanatical, Leninist, but also as Chinese nationalist, Communists. Above all, war-weariness joined nationalism to make Mao the preferred leader, if only because his coming to power promised to end the civil war and reunify China—as, after all, it did.

American Reaction

American policy was indecisive. Alone among the great powers the United States had tried to make China also a great power, largely overestimating its capacities and American long-range willingness to commit its own resources toward this goal. The United States underestimated the communism of Mao—he was no mere "agrarian reformer," as some Americans thought. Conversely, the United States overestimated Mao's ties with the Russians. He had come to power not at their command but, if anything, in spite of it; and the scars of Stalin's 1927 failure in China remained to remind him that Russia's interests were far from identical with China's. Worst of all, after Mao came to power, as a result of strong Soviet-American antagonism and Mao's intervention in the Korean War, Washington's attitude toward Mao came to be dominated by the false conviction that he was essentially a Soviet agent and that Communist China was and would remain another Soviet satellite. (True, Chinese Communist public statements at that time were firmly pro-Soviet, but a few acute American observers saw behind them.)

Washington's essential bafflement with postwar China was never better revealed than in the contradictions between its expressed views about the Chinese Nationalists and Communists and its actions toward them. During World War II the United States pressed Chiang toward reforms and simultaneously supported him sufficiently, because of its preoccupation with the Japanese, so that he did not feel compelled to carry them through. Moreover, the United States viewed the Chinese Communists with much the same equanimity—conservatives like Ambassador Hurley just as much as leftists—as it did the Soviet Communists. After the war the United States transported and supported the Chinese Nationalist armies enough to alienate the Communists completely, but not enough to turn the tide in their favor. Then, in General Marshall's attempt at mediation, Washington treated Chiang and Mao as equals, thus antagonizing both. When this mediation failed, as it had to, the United States in effect left Chiang to his own devices, only to pick him up again in Taiwan once he was completely defeated.

Behind all this record of mistakes lay the initial romanticized American picture of Chiang, a demonized picture of Mao, illusions about Stalin, and, most crucially, the unwillingness of the American people to face up to the choice or to choose decisively, once the choice had to be made, between major American intervention in Chiang's favor or total abandonment of him. The United States did neither—and is still suffering therefrom.

Finally, once Mao did come to power, Washington continued to support Chiang on Taiwan, and after the Korean War and the Chinese intervention therein, the United States shielded Chiang with its naval and air power, thus almost guaranteeing Sino-American hostility, since any powerful China would insist on territorial unity, including Taiwan.

The reemergence of a powerful, united China—that it was Communist was perhaps of secondary significance—in 1949 and thereafter marked a change in the Asian balance of power comparable only to the advance of the Red Army and of Soviet power to the Elbe and the resultant division of Germany. Historically, as we have seen, American policy toward China had tried to prevent that country, and therefore

East Asia, from being dominated by any single hostile power and to preserve the outlets of American commercial interests there. To prevent these developments it had fought and defeated Japan.

With the reemergence of at least a potentially strong and clearly hostile China, and all the more so because it seemed to Washington to be a close subordinate of a hostile Soviet Union, American policy became inevitably hostile to it. Nor, probably, could this have been avoided. After all, East and Southeast Asia had for centuries been essentially dominated by Imperial China, before its own decline and then the rise of Imperial Japan. Insofar as Washington was to continue to pursue its, and Great Britain's, traditional policy of preventing any such domination, *any* strong, united, expansionist China could hardly become its firm ally—indeed, was more likely to become its enemy.

Mao's Position.   Stalin had aided Mao in 1945 as Roosevelt had aided Chiang; but it is doubtful that the Soviet dictator ever wanted China to become completely Communist. He always feared that another Communist leader could, and therefore would, defy him—it was for this reason that he had excommunicated Tito—and he most probably neither anticipated nor desired the revival of a strong China, Communist or not. As he well knew, China had territorial grievances against Russia. Moreover, Mao had come to power in 1935 not, like all his predecessors, as a result of a Soviet fiat; and although he had thereafter on the surface conformed to the Soviet line, Stalin had little reason to believe that he would remain indefinitely and completely faithful to Moscow.

Nevertheless, until the collapse of the Sino-Soviet alliance in 1959, Mao was an ally of Moscow above all else, in addition to ideological ties, because he remained, as he still does today, a bitter enemy of the United States. For Mao the United States was not only one of the "imperialist exploiters" of China—and in 1949 the most powerful of them—but also (worse) it was the chief ally and supporter of Chiang.

The precipitous collapse of Chiang and his forces in 1949 showed that the "mandate of Heaven" had clearly been transferred to Mao; and he and his associates were greeted, upon their accession to power, by near universal support. The Chinese intellectuals and, one may assume, the Chinese peasantry as well were weary of civil war, outraged about the weakness of and Western penetration into China, and prepared to give the benefit of the doubt to, and in their majority to support, new Chinese leadership which promised peace, strong central government, economic development, and a nationalist policy.

Mao needed economic aid for development, and, after long negotiations with Stalin in Moscow in 1949-50, he got some—one more reason to "lean to one side" (the Soviet), as he put it. But, as the future was to show, Stalin was right; Mao was a nationalist as well as a communist, as Stalin's successors were to learn to their disadvantage.

THE KOREAN WAR

Stalin's forward foreign policy did not end with the termination of the Berlin Blockade. On the contrary, to the United States and the West in general the Korean War, which began in 1950 with a North Korean invasion of South Korea, seemed an intensification of the Soviet expansionism which had manifested itself mainly in the Prague coup and the Berlin Blockade. Again, the verdict of history will probably be more differentiated and complex than a simple one of Soviet expansionism.

The United States had withdrawn its troops from South Korea, and its officials, notably Secretary of State Acheson, had indicated that South Korea was not within the American defense perimeter in the Pacific. Thus Stalin could have thought that intervention by the United States was at least far from certain. But he could hardly have held it to be impossible—after all, the American stands in Azerbaijan, the Greek civil war, and the Berlin Blockade were firm enough, and their molder, President Truman, was still in office. North Korea, expansionist and extremist, had probably been the main initiator of the war; yet, the government at Pyongyang would hardly have dared to move without a commitment of Soviet support. Moreover, a Communist overrunning of South Korea would menace the United States position in Japan, the great prize of war in the Pacific. One may perhaps conclude that Stalin was willing to support the North Korean move with material aid but not with military action; that is, it was a limited, carefully measured Soviet probe against the United States. Yet, in the last analysis it was expansionist, at least potentially, on the part of Stalin: like the Berlin Blockade, it was—out of whatever motive—an attempt to change by force the "truce lines" of World War II.

President Truman reacted firmly and forcibly. His initial commitment of men and material was just enough to prevent the American and South Korean troops from being driven into the sea. Then, through General MacArthur's brilliantly executed landing at Inchon, outflanking the North Korean forces, the American troops, which had been joined by symbolic contingents from the Western members of the United Nations (Soviet boycotts of the Security Council meetings having, providentially for the United States, enabled Washington to fashion a UN umbrella for its operations,) swept northward and retook the South Korean capital of Seoul. They moved over the zonal boundary into North Korea with the expressed aim of "liberating" and "unifying" all of Korea, clearly under a non-Communist government—changing the "truce lines" in favor of the United States.

At this point the Chinese Communists—in the guise of "volunteers"—intervened, after having vainly warned the United States, via the Indians, that they would do so if American forces crossed into North Korea. MacArthur's troops, largely because he had neither foreseen nor properly prepared for Chinese intervention, suffered a major defeat and were again pushed back to the south, only to rebound, recapture Seoul again, and push north to near the parallel. Then Stalin's death in March 1953 intervened, and the long truce negotiations began.

BACK TO EUROPE

The Korean War greatly activated United States policy in the Far East, most notably by the guarantee for, and alliance with, Chiang's government on Taiwan, and more by the great general increase in American military forces and expenditures, in particular, in the Asian theater. It was also primarily responsible for the extensive aid given by Washington to the French struggle against Ho Chi Minh and his Vietminh Communist guerrillas in Indochina. Moreover, it contributed further to the postwar economic recovery of Japan and to the closeness of United States-Japanese relations.

It also had profound reverberations in Europe. For most Americans, and certainly for their government, the Russian-supported and Russian-supplied attack on South Korea was essentially a Soviet move, and it made dangerously likely a Soviet attack on Western Europe. The Chinese intervention only strengthened this view of the war, since Peking was then wrongly considered as simply the largest of the Soviet satellites.

Nor was this view of the Korean War peculiar to Americans; its outbreak led to widespread alarm, for example, in West Germany, and the British and French governments were also seriously concerned. Both the United States and the Western European powers, therefore, were united in their estimate of the greatly increased Soviet danger and of the urgent necessity of establishing a military barrier against it in Western Europe. This led directly to the establishment of the North Atlantic Treaty Organization (NATO), and, perhaps even more importantly, to the rearmament of West Germany.

The American decision in 1947-48 had, as we have seen, led first to the economic and then to the political unity of the three western zones of Germany. In 1949 Dr. Konrad Adenauer, the head of the new Christian Democratic party, was elected first chancellor of the German Federal Republic. Simultaneously, his economics minister, Dr. Ludwig Erhard, instituted a combination of market economy and welfare state which soon brought to West Germany a high level of prosperity. Adenauer was determined to rearm Germany, for two reasons: first, to assure its protection against the Red Army, and, second, to give it military and thus political power in Western Europe. He was also determined to bring about Western European unity, and with his fellow Catholics Robert Schuman, long the French foreign minister, and Alcide de Gasperi, the Italian premier, he made much progress toward that goal, with strong and constant American encouragement and support.

Meanwhile, the new West German Bundeswehr was formed; several more American infantry divisions were sent to Europe, with General Eisenhower as the first supreme NATO commander; a Western-Europe-wide United States-financed supply and communications network was set up; and the Western military position there became thus more favorable.

The Russians could not, of course, be expected to remain indifferent to these developments, which caused a major shift in the European balance of power to their disfavor. What their policy in postwar Germany had been primarily designed to prevent—the reunification, economic power, and rearmament of the western zones of Germany, in alliance with the United States against the Soviet Union—had now become reality. True, the Soviets had acquired first the atomic and then the hydrogen bomb, thus guaranteeing their own security and ending the short period of American unilateral atomic predominance. Moreover, insofar as their alliance with China continued, they were the stronger because China's successful holding off of United States forces in the Korean War had greatly strengthened the Chinese military potential. But the exertions necessary for supporting the Korean War had seriously strained the Soviet, and even more the East European, economies. Finally, Stalin in his last years was increasingly obsessed by pathological—indeed, paranoic—persecution manias. Actually, the announcement in early 1953, a few weeks before his death, of the "Doctors' Plot," an allegedly American-Yugoslav-Israeli-inspired plot by Stalin's doctors to kill him, probably presaged a new great purge. Then, in March 1953, he died.

RUSSIA AND EASTERN EUROPE AFTER STALIN

The impact of Stalin's death was to be profoundly felt all over the world. His successors, first Malenkov and later Khrushchev, felt compelled to undertake a major program of liberalization, both at home and in the Soviet sphere in Eastern Europe. At home, they shot the secret-police chief Beria, who had unsuccessfully aspired to the succession; and in addition to struggling among themselves, which led in 1955 to Khrushchev's supremacy, they released the millions of prisoners in the slave labor camps, curbed the powers of the secret police, pumped more consumer goods into the economy, and gave certain limited possibilities for expression to the cowed intellectuals, while maintaining firm party control over the commanding heights of Soviet life.

In the Soviet Union itself, these reforms led to a significant decline in popular discontent. Simultaneously, the post-Stalin rulers pushed forward vigorously with Soviet military strength, and gave priority to strategic nuclear weapons while cutting down the ground forces. (In these years—1953-56—the foundations were laid for the great Soviet missile and space successes of the late 1950s and 1960s.)

But in Eastern Europe the results of the Khrushchev liberalization measures were very different: they led to general ferment and dissent and in 1956 to the coming to power of Gomułka in Poland and to the Hungarian Revolution. The fundamental reason for these Soviet defeats was the rising force of East European nationalism, fired by economic privation and intellectual discontent. With the exception of Yugoslavia and Albania, communism had come to Eastern Europe on the bayonets of the Red Army. Moreover, with the exception of Bulgaria and, partially, of Czechoslovakia, Eastern Europe had been traditionally anti-Russian, the local Communist parties small, alienated sects, and nationalism endemic and proud. Thus communism in Eastern Europe went against nationalism, religion, peasant desire for the land, workers' desires for sharing the fruits of their work, and intellectual nonconformism. No wonder that once the fog of terror over the area was lifted, discontent became rampant.

It reached its height in the two countries, Poland and Hungary, which contained the strongest and most anti-Russian nationalism, hated Communist regimes, and had many precedents for intellectual discontent. Communism in Poland was saved in October 1956 by Khrushchev's reluctant acquiescence to Gomułka, and by the latter's determination to make Polish communism more autonomous and less tyrannical, but, all the same, to keep it in power and to keep Poland an ally, if no longer a total satellite, of the Soviet Union. In Hungary the Communists were few and sectarian, and their leaders rash and tyrannical. The rebellious intellectuals and the nationalistic population, on the other hand, infected by the news of the Polish events, broke forth in October 1956 in elemental revolutionary power, only to be crushed by the Red Army. Imre Nagy, the revolution's reluctant leader, a much nobler man but a much less skillful statesman than Gomułka, paid with his life for his preference for patriotism over Stalinism.

The Rumanian and Bulgarian Communists, combining Byzantine heritage with ruthlessness, kept the lid on their few rebellious intellectuals. Ulbricht in East Germany, whose regime had been saved on June 17, 1953 by Red Army tanks from the flash revolt which would otherwise have toppled him, strangled the 1956 dissent in East Germany at birth. Novotný in Prague did much the same. The East Germans, having risen in 1953, had no taste for another unsuccessful rebellion; the Czechs were as yet too cautious, and not yet poor enough, to rise. Thereafter, Kádár in Budapest and Gomułka in Warsaw slowly but surely reconsolidated their power, and Khrushchev was wise enough to allow Gomułka to keep, and gradually to grant to the other East European rulers, considerable autonomy as long as they remained faithful political and military allies of the Soviet Union.

4

Eisenhower, Khrushchev, and Mao

The war hero General Dwight Eisenhower in 1953 became President of the United States and remained so for the following eight years. He saw his task at home as one of consolidation and mediation in order to calm the domestic strains which had been aroused by the fall of China and the Korean War. Abroad, he was fundamentally a man of peace, and at the end of his administration he proved ready to reciprocate Khrushchev's moves toward a U.S.-USSR détente. Yet, until 1959 his Secretary of State was John Foster Dulles, a Puritan international lawyer whose secular religion was anti-communism, who seemed determined to line up as many powers as possible throughout the whole world in alliances against the Soviet Union, and who regarded neutralism as something almost sinful. Given the atmosphere of the time and, in particular, the impact of the Korean War, it was perhaps understandable that Dulles was as dogmatic as he was; and he certainly always felt menaced from his right by extreme reactionaries, notably Senator Joseph McCarthy, who briefly elevated demagogic anti-communism into a fanatical ideology.

Yet Dulles's bark was much worse than his bite; and Eisenhower was determined to avoid war. When the East Germans rose in June 1953, on the other side of the Brandenburg Gate from American troops, the United States remained passive—albeit perhaps more out of surprise than by design. American passivity in the Hungarian Revolution was, to the Russians, the East European Communists, and the world, a clear sign that the United States would not challenge the Soviet Union militarily within the borders of its postwar gains in Europe. (Indeed, it may well have been one of the antecedents of East European liberalization in the 1960s.) Moreover, Eisenhower brought peace in the Korean War by accepting the *status quo ante;* that is, the continuation of the partition of the country. (He got the Chinese to agree to the truce, it should be noted, by credibly threatening them with atomic bombardment if they did not.) Also, when in 1954 the fall of Dien Bien Phu, in Indochina, seemed imminent and when Dulles, Vice-President Nixon, and Chairman of the Joint Chiefs Admiral Radford all recommended American military intervention to save the beleaguered French, Eisenhower decided to stay out. Thereupon, the French made peace, with the reluctant consent of the United States, and Vietnam was partitioned.

From the hindsight of the late 1960s, one may well feel that Eisenhower was unwise, thereafter, to displace the French as the protector of the new nationalist regime of Ngo Dinh Diem in Saigon. But there is no reason to assume that Eisenhower or Dulles anticipated anything like the subsequent developments in that tortured land.

THE BEGINNINGS OF SOVIET-AMERICAN DÉTENTE

Most important, perhaps, was the slow, often interrupted, but persistently pursued search by both Washington and Moscow toward détente, toward a limitation of their conflict relationship. This first became symbolically apparent at the 1955 Geneva summit conference, when Eisenhower and Bulganin both declared that Soviet-American war was out of the question.

The new Russian leaders had made it clear from the moment that they came to power that they were searching for some means of lowering the level of hostility in their relations with the West. Why did they so act? Primarily, it seems, for the same reason that Eisenhower did: the overriding priority of ensuring against the awful destruction of nuclear war. The acquisition of mutually destructive nuclear weapons by the United States and the Soviet Union has had one major consequence: by making the cost of war so enormous, it has preserved the peace between the two superpowers and thereby avoided another world war. Had it not been for atomic weapons, it is at least doubtful if the Berlin crisis, the Korean War, and the Vietnam War would have remained as limited as they did. In any case, as thermonuclear weapons became ever more effective, and as the Soviet Union as well as the United States obtained intercontinental thermonuclear delivery capability, the danger of war by accident or escalation became greater, and both Washington and Moscow were therefore more anxious than before to lower the temperature of their confrontation.

There was one other significant reason from the Soviet side: the desire of Stalin's successors to concentrate on their domestic and imperial problems without being compelled to occupy themselves simultaneously with a confrontation with the United States. Conversely, Eisenhower personally, and the American government in general, inclined toward reciprocating Soviet proposals for détente if only because public opinion at home and abroad made it so difficult for them to do otherwise.

By the late 1950s another increasingly significant factor had arisen in Soviet foreign policy calculations which added to

Moscow's impetus for détente: the approaching Sino-Soviet split. Moscow naturally did not wish two confrontations at once. Moreover, the United States was, as it remains, essentially a status quo power, while Maoist China is an expansionist one, both geopolitically and ideologically. Thus Moscow was the more inclined to improve its relations with Washington, insofar as its conflict with Peking did not, out of competition in militancy, prevent this, in order to prevent a rapprochement between its two enemies, Washington and Peking, or, at least, to make Washington less hostile to Soviet policies.

THE SINO-SOVIET SPLIT

The slowness with which the West realized the deterioration and collapse of the Sino-Soviet alliance in the 1950s makes one inclined to believe that the myth of proletarian internationalism remained alive longer in the minds of its capitalist opponents than in the beliefs and actions of its professed supporters. We now know that relations between Stalin and Mao, although not bad, were never cordial, dating back to Stalin's blunders with Chinese communism in the 1920s. When Mao, most probably contrary to Stalin's hopes, came to power over all of China, there ensued much hard bargaining, aided, of course, by Washington's hostility to the new Chinese leaders, before the Sino-Soviet alliance was in 1950 put on what seemed a firm footing. Yet, Stalin retained most of his postwar foothold in China (bases at Port Arthur and Dairen), very likely intrigued with the later purged Chinese Communist boss of Manchuria, Kao Kang, against Mao, and hardly gave China the all-out support in the Korean War which it must have hoped for. Even so, the need for Soviet economic and military assistance, the hostility of Washington, and the necessity to wait until its power was fully consolidated throughout China, plus, one may well now assume, differences within the Chinese Communist leadership itself over the question, delayed any serious outbreak of Sino-Soviet hostility until after Stalin's death.

Despite all that they had against him, Mao and his associates probably preferred Stalin's policies to Khrushchev's. The latter liberalized at home, improved relations with the United States, and made concessions to East European unrest —none were policies which Mao could view with favor. Conversely, the stronger the new Chinese regime became and the more it asserted its own foreign policy, the less likely could Khrushchev have been expected to view it with favor.

We still know little about the true nature of Sino-Soviet relations in the early and mid-1950s, immediately before and after the death of Stalin. It is significant that the first visit abroad of the new Soviet leaders, Khrushchev and Bulganin, in 1954, was to Peking, where they made significant concessions to Mao, including surrendering their privileges at Port Arthur, Dairen, and in Sinkiang—undoubtedly in the hope of improving what must have already been the strained state of Sino-Soviet relations. But the indications given by Malenkov, Stalin's first successor, and then by Khrushchev that the new leadership wanted a détente with the United States, its liberalization at home, and, perhaps most importantly, its great loss of prestige as a result of the 1956 Polish and Hungarian events, plus the subsequent trip of Chinese premier Chou En-lai to Eastern Europe, almost as if he were acting as a mediator between Moscow and its rebellious client states there, all contributed to the beginning of the Sino-Soviet dispute.

The Chinese were the more affronted by these Soviet domestic and foreign moves toward liberalization because Khrushchev, like Stalin, proclaimed them in the guise of ideological formulae which inevitably seemed to give them general validity, for China as well. It was as though the new Soviet leader were claiming to control not only East European, but also Chinese, policies. Mao, who after Stalin's death, with considerable reason, probably considered himself the greatest living Marxist-Leninist statesman and, therefore, ideologist, was simply not prepared to accept such an imposition.

Stalin had paid relatively little attention to the rising independent states in the underdeveloped, third world—for him all non-Communists were anathema anyway. But Khrushchev was determined to conduct a more flexible policy there, trying to use political influence acquired by economic and military aid to bring radical, albeit non-Communist, leaders like Nasser, Sukarno, and even Nehru over to his side, thus detaching them from the United States. By the mid-1950s China was also beginning to move into the same third world by political and economic means; indeed, at the 1955 Bandung conference of third world statesmen, Chou En-lai scored a great success for China by his subtle diplomacy and moderation.

Nor was Khrushchev willing to give East and Southeast Asia to the Chinese as a sphere of influence, any more than Stalin had been willing to give them to Imperial Japan. The Soviet Union, an Asia power, intended to maintain, and if possible to increase, its influence there. India, the largest underdeveloped state except China, bordering on both the Soviet Union and China and trying to keep good relations with them both and with the United States, was the most important area of Sino-Soviet geopolitical conflict in Asia.

Another such area was in China itself. The far western Chinese province of Sinkiang, formerly called Chinese Turkestan, contained a great majority of inhabitants who were not ethnic Chinese but Turkic nomadic tribesmen, closely related to those over the border in Soviet Central Asia. Sinkiang had earlier been a subject of Russo-Chinese controversy; until 1949 it had been under Soviet influence; and its importance was now greatly increased by the discovery there of large amounts of uranium, essential for the beginning Chinese atomic energy program.

The Military-Atomic Conflict

This was another major source of Sino-Soviet conflict—the military, and especially the atomic area. China needed modern weapons and wanted, above all, atomic ones, the sign and requirement of a superpower, which Mao was determined to make China into, so that she could recover her traditional hegemony in East and Southeast Asia and deal on equal terms with Washington and Moscow. Her participation in the Korean War modernized her army, through her receipt of Soviet weapons (for which, she later charged, Moscow tried to collect payment), and her fight to a standstill with the United States (as it seemed not only to China but to much of the world) greatly increased her military prestige. Yet, military technology, especially in the fields of nuclear weapons and guided missiles, was rushing forward rapidly, and China, like France before as well as under de Gaulle, was determined to acquire nuclear missile capability. That she did so is not surprising; what is amazing—indeed, in retrospect it may well have been his greatest mistake—was Khrushchev's initial willingness to give China some atomic assistance; something, after all, that the United States has never given to any of its allies.

The first serious Sino-Soviet confrontation was at a Communist summit meeting in Moscow in November 1957—the fortieth anniversary of the Bolshevik Revolution. The meeting was secret; only recently, from Chinese revelations, have we learned that Mao and Khrushchev had some serious disputes there. They were ostensibly largely over the issue of "peaceful transition to socialism"—the coming to power of communism without a violent revolution—but actually, we may assume, they really disagreed over most of the issues outlined above, and in particular over the one which combined the issues of policies toward the United States and the third world: the appropriate level of risk-taking for the Soviet Union (not for China, which was still too weak) vis-à-vis the

United States with respect to giving military support to China and to "national liberation wars." Indeed, in the largest sense the issue of policy toward the United States was as important, if not more important, than any other. Mao was determined to conquer Taiwan and the offshore islands, while Khrushchev was determined not to risk war with the United States in order to aid China in this.

But the atomic and military issue must also have been much in evidence. Just before the 1957 conference the Russians had launched their first Sputnik, thus indicating that they were ahead in the space race, greatly lifting their own prestige, and lowering that of the United States. (The shock of this in the United States led to a major program of rearmament and eventually contributed to American strategic superiority in the 1960 s.) Mao interpreted this to mean that "the east wind is prevailing over the west"; in other words, that Khrushchev should take more risks vis-à-vis the United States instead of cultivating it. More important was the factor which presumably led to the summit meeting coming to at least formal agreement: just before it Moscow signed a new military agreement with Peking which promised some help— how much or what kind we do not know—toward China's gaining an atomic capability.

The Soviets thereafter, in 1958 and 1959, did give the Chinese significant aid in designing and building nuclear reactors, separation plants, and the like. But this must, from the Chinese view, have been far from sufficient and much less than what they felt they had been led to expect. Already by the spring of 1958 Chinese statements indicated their feeling that they had been deceived by the Russians and that fundamentally they would have to rely upon their own resources for obtaining military superpower status.

At the same time Chinese internal policy, which had gone through a brief, ill-fated period of liberalization (the so-called "hundred flowers" period), was reversed by Mao personally, apparently against the at least partial opposition of many of his closest associates, including his heir-apparent, Liu Shao-ch'i; the party secretary-general, Teng Hsiao-p'ing; and the minister of defense, Marshal P'eng Te-huai. Thus in 1958 began the "Great Leap Forward"—essentially a plan to bring about rapid, forced-draft industrialization in China without relying on foreign aid, Soviet or otherwise. It also had a strong utopian component in the so-called "people's communes"—vast, largely agrarian groups of people who lived, ate, and slept communally, for whom Communist enthusiasm was supposed to substitute for material incentives in raising agricultural and industrial production.

By 1960 the Great Leap had failed to meet either its economic or its ideological objects. "Backyard steel mills" had not worked; Chinese agriculture had been disorganized; large-scale food shortages had occurred; massive famine was averted only by major imports of grain from Canada and Australia; and the Chinese Communist party was in considerable disarray—more, we now know, than seemed at the time. Thus China's internal problems had increased. So, however, had Mao's fanaticism abroad, for several reasons, involving primarily the Taiwan and offshore island (Quemoy and Matsu) issues and his relations with India. With respect to these, Khrushchev refused to follow but, instead, opposed Mao's policies.

KHRUSHCHEV'S FORWARD STRATEGY

Khrushchev's opposition was not only—indeed, not primarily—because the Soviet leader was, in contrast to Mao, determined to come to terms with Washington, let alone on American terms. On the contrary, Khrushchev, like Mao, had drawn from his Sputnik successes, from the relatively rapid and successful reconsolidation of his position in Eastern Europe, and from his successes in the third world—notably in Egypt and Indonesia, the conclusion that the balance of power was turning in favor of the Soviet Union and that he was properly entitled to take advantage of this by improving his position vis-à-vis Washington.

That is to say, he was now prepared to take some risks, perhaps even, as the 1962 Cuban missile crisis was to show, as great ones as Mao wanted him to—but for Soviet, not Chinese, advantage. He refused to take any major risks in order to help China to get possession of Quemoy and Matsu, to say nothing of Taiwan, and thus the crises over these islands in the mid- and late-1950s subsided with Washington the victor. Nor was he prepared to take the side of China against India, since this would only guarantee that Russian gains in India would be replaced at best by American ones and at worst by Chinese, with the balance of power in the area tipped sharply in favor of China.

What Khrushchev did decide was to improve his position in Europe. True, by 1957-58 it was not as bad as in 1956. Gomułka had reconsolidated his and communism's power in Poland, suppressed his revisionist dissidents, and remained a close and faithful ally of Moscow's. Khrushchev had occupied and silenced Hungary. The lesser dissidence in the other East European states seemed to him safely under control. However, as we now know—but the West did not then suspect—both Albania and Rumania were beginning to maneuver to escape from Soviet control. But in 1958 this was just beginning and Khrushchev could hardly as yet have found it alarming: indeed, 1958 was the year that he took Russian troops out of Rumania—a move he was to live to regret. Yugoslavia, again drifting away from the Soviet line, clearly did not wish to break completely with Moscow. On the contrary, China—and Albania—were denouncing Yugoslavia far more violently than were the Russians. Most serious for Khrushchev, East Germany was by 1958 in serious trouble, not so much internally as because of West Berlin.

As West German prosperity continued to rise, and as after 1956 Ulbricht cracked down still more on his rebellious subjects, notably by beginning a full agricultural collectivization program, the flight of refugees out of East Germany through West Berlin—where the border between West and East Berlin was, according to four-power agreement, open— became greater and greater. Some way, Ulbricht kept pressing Moscow, had to be found to stanch this running wound, or else East Germany would become economically unviable.

Thus Khrushchev had a serious defensive problem with respect to East Germany; if he did nothing about it, not only Ulbricht's but also his own position would suffer. But he had, he felt, an offensive opportunity in West Germany as well. West Berlin lay isolated, except for the air, road, and rail corridors, in the middle of East Germany. West Germany, where Konrad Adenauer still ruled, was getting stronger all the time. Moreover, in the course of Eisenhower's "new look" in defense policy—what his Secretary of Defense "Engine Charlie" Wilson termed "more bang for the buck"—the Americans had decided to introduce tactical nuclear weapons in large numbers into West Germany, thereby counterbalancing the Red Army's numerical superiority. What for the Russians must have seemed a far more dangerous move was the American decision to arm the West German army and air force with these tactical nuclear weapons. True, the United States kept its sole control over their use. Nevertheless, the West German Bundeswehr had thus become the third nuclear power in the world in terms of the amount of its atomic arms —although not of its control over them. This must also have contributed toward Khrushchev's maximum aim: to push back American and West German prestige, and increase that of the Soviets, so that the potential Western military pressure on Russia's western flank would be eased. (It hardly need be added that he must have found this particularly desirable when it increasingly appeared that he might have to engage in a major long-term struggle with Mao on his eastern flank.)

It is important to understand the true complexity of the Soviet and American positions in Germany, and particularly in Berlin. West Berlin, as long as refugees could stream into

it from East Germany, by its very existence automatically de-
stabilized East Germany. Yet, any successful Soviet move
against this danger, by forcing an American withdrawal,
would destabilize West Germany, whose security, its leaders
and citizens were convinced, depended upon a credible United
States guarantee. In short, any change in the German status
quo would destabilize Soviet-American relations. Khrushchev
was, therefore, playing with fire in Berlin, as Stalin had in
1948-49; and this fact, of which he was clearly aware, ex-
plained his long delays and postponements of decisions during
the whole crisis. Nevertheless, by the end of 1958 he had
reluctantly come to the conclusion that something had to be
done. In November he demanded that West Berlin be made
a free city without Western troops and threatened that if
this were not done he would sign a peace treaty with East
Germany and thereby end the Allied rights of access to West
Berlin.

The Western, and particularly the American, reaction
was essentially firm, although expressing willingness to ne-
gotiate on the whole German problem. Thereafter, the crisis
dragged on at varying degrees of severity. It did result—and
this was in the long run its greatest effect—in a major speed-
ing up of American armament programs, notably after President Kennedy took office in 1961, including conventional as
well as nuclear weapons. Much had been made in the United
States in the late 1950s, notably, of course, by the Democratic
opposition, of the "missile gap"—of the danger that Moscow
would catch up and overtake the United States in strategic
ICBM capability. Whether it could have or not, it did not—
rather, the Russians built some 700 medium-range missiles
targeted on Western Europe.

SINO-SOVIET RELATIONS: THE POINT OF NO RETURN

By 1959, then, Khrushchev was in fact engaged on two
fronts; on the west, against the United States in West Berlin,

and on the east against Mao. It would have required all the skill of a Bismarck to have won on one or both—in fact he did not win on either. He wanted to force the United States out of West Berlin, yet, at the same time he could not afford the risk of nuclear war. Trying to combine both these aims, he visited the United States in 1959, and at the Camp David conversations with President Eisenhower gained only very little on the Berlin issue (enough, though, to alarm Adenauer and push him toward the willing arms of de Gaulle); but he lost far more thereby with the Chinese, who saw in his visit the proof that he would give them no effective aid against the Americans in East Asia.

However, the immediate causes of the "point of no return" in Sino-Soviet relations—the point after which both sides anticipated a break rather than reconciliation—were three other ones: the Soviet withdrawal of atomic aid to Peking, the Soviet refusal to support the Chinese position on India, and the unsuccessful attempt by Khrushchev to intrigue within the Chinese leadership against Mao.

Sino-Soviet relations had been worsening throughout 1958 and early 1959. In June of 1959, as we learned only much later, the Soviets formally cancelled their agreement to give China atomic aid. In August of that year the Chinese initiated the first meaningful series of border incidents on their frontier with India, in Ladakh, where in territory disputed between Delhi and Peking the Chinese had been building an important strategic road from Sinkiang into Tibet and the Indians had clumsily begun to try to cut them off. (The Chinese were also enraged at Nehru's giving asylum in India to the fugitive Dalai Lama, subsequent to Peking's crushing of the Tibetan rebellion earlier that year.) In spite of Peking's efforts to the contrary, the Russians issued a statement making quite clear their neutrality toward China and India with respect to the border incidents.

Presumably, it was primarily because of the issue of atomic aid, however, that the Soviets were able to gain some support within the Chinese leadership, notably that of the defense minister Marshal P'eng Te-huai. It was natural that the Chinese Army would want the most modern weapons in case of a conflict with the Americans, and only from Moscow could they obtain atomic aid rapidly. P'eng was probably also opposed to the Great Leap, as Liu and Teng were as well. In any case, at the Lushan Plenum in September 1959 a confrontation took place between Mao and P'eng, and Mao's victory resulted in the latter being removed, along with his associates. What position Liu and Teng took at the Plenum we do not know; but in the light of developments during the later Cultural Revolution one may assume that they were not total supporters of Mao.

For Khrushchev and Mao the die was now cast. It is important to realize how early this occurred—indeed, at a time, September 1959, when the great majority of Western experts and their governments did not really believe that there were any serious differences at all.

Once the breach occurred, much more followed: Mao became convinced that Khrushchev was betraying not only orthodox Marxism-Leninism—and, therefore, that henceforth Peking, not Moscow, incarnated it—and also that Khrushchev was betraying not only "the revolution," but also Chinese, and, indeed, Russian, national interests to the Americans. From that time, revived Chinese chauvinism reinforced ideological fanaticism to such an extent that Mao determined to have Peking replace Moscow as the Mecca, the one source of orthodoxy and legitimacy, and, therefore, of command, in world communism.

Public expression of great-power hostility at the ideological level added—to the relatively discreet, and even possibly compromisable, specific issues—the element of secular, universal, uncompromisable, and absolute hostility. And because communism was a secular religion and a split in it comparable to the religious wars in seventeenth-century Europe, it provided a built-in factor of escalation to the controversy:

it guaranteed that each side would try to subvert the other's allies and that the Russians would try to defend, and the Chinese to acquire supremacy over, the international Communist movement and, indeed, the whole Communist plus radical-nationalist world.

Initially, Mao began this conflict, since Khrushchev represented the status quo and he the challenger. From 1960, when the Sino-Soviet controversy first, albeit in an esoteric form, became public, until 1965, Sino-Soviet hostility outwardly displayed itself in a cyclical manner—a cycle of extreme hostility, followed by another cycle of at least ostensible attempts at agreement. But this was merely the surface image; in fact, these cycles represented only tactical moves on the part of Moscow and Peking, each trying to gain support thereby among other Communist parties. Until the fall of Khrushchev in late 1964, the Chinese appeared to be on the offensive, and, indeed, they gained much, but largely because of the inflexible tactics of the Russians, who seemed to demand that all Communist states and parties choose completely and totally between Moscow and Peking. In other words, Khrushchev, like John Foster Dulles, refused to accept neutralism in his own sphere. Moreover, he constantly and unsuccessfully tried to mobilize his Communist allies, hesitating or not, against the danger from Maoist heresy. In the process—and far more damaging for the Russian cause—he felt himself reluctantly compelled to make such concessions in the course of his attempts at mobilization to such reluctant allies as the Italians, the Rumanians, and the Yugoslavs that he ended up not only without any effective mobilization but with a far looser, less united, more pluralistic Communist world. In sum, then, Khrushchev's attempts to reunite the Communist world produced only the opposite of his aims—they furthered pluralism and destroyed unity even more.

The Chinese, initially, were far more clever. Realizing the error of the Russians' attempts to restore what was lost—the unity of the Communist world—they were only too ready to profit thereby. They did not press for total conformity; on the contrary, they seemed willing to accept even neutrality, or—in the case of the Rumanians—only partial support. They were, temporarily, very wise to do this; but only temporarily, because many of the parties who in the early 1960s seemed to be supporting or at least to be neutral toward the Chinese were in fact merely furthering their own interests. And these interests were neither Soviet nor Chinese. On the contrary, as we shall see, the main result of the Sino-Soviet conflict was not a shift of loyalties from Moscow to Peking but rather a disaster for both the Russians and the Chinese: increasing pluralism in the Communist and the underdeveloped world; gradual, sometimes almost imperceptible, always increasing escape of a growing number of Communist parties and states from both Moscow and Peking in the direction of more independence. Ours is an age of nationalism, nowhere more strikingly, in recent years, than in the Communist world itself.

The Importance of Albania

Initially, however, this trend toward Communist pluralism certainly benefited the Chinese, and, it is important to note, the Americans as well. In mid-1960 it became clear, as had been foreshadowed although not realized by the West for some years before, that Albania had successfully exchanged Soviet domination for Chinese influence and economic aid. The explanation for this was fairly simple: since its independence, just before World War I, Albania had been threatened with partition by its three neighbors, Yugoslavia, Greece, and Italy, and maintained its independence only as long as none of them was strong enough, or all could not agree, to partition it. The Albanian partisan guerrillas, led by Enver Hoxha, won their victory in World War II under Yugoslav tutelage and control. They escaped this in 1948 by revolting, given the advantage of the Soviet-Yugoslav break, in favor of Soviet hegemony. When, first briefly and inconclusively in 1955 and then more clearly in 1959, Khrushchev moved toward reconciliation with Belgrade, and therefore inevitably toward sacrificing Hoxha's interests for Tito's, it was only natural that the Albanians would look for a protector even farther away—meaning less danger to their independence—than Khrushchev; and they found one in Mao. Moreover, their own underdevelopment made their regime necessarily extreme, just as China's did for Mao's regime; internal policy, therefore, combined with external interest to cement the Sino-Albanian alliance—the first time since Genghis Khan that an East Asian power had predominant influence over any state in Europe.

The importance of a pro-Chinese Albania was much greater than it might have seemed: from Mao's viewpoint it symbolized the worldwide nature of the Chinese challenge to Soviet authority and influence. If China could have predominant influence over a Communist state on the Adriatic, where would Khrushchev not encounter Peking's challenge? His efforts to subvert and overthrow Hoxha failed miserably; indeed, their only effect was to accentuate the worsening of Sino-Soviet relations.

China had also brought to its side the ethnically Chinese Communist parties in Southeast Asia—Burma, Thailand, and Malaya. Moreover, it had partially drawn away from Moscow those East and Southeast Asian parties which were particularly anti-American and which thereby necessarily opposed Khrushchev's attempts at rapprochement with Washington: the Indonesian, North Vietnamese, and North Korean parties, and, after it split, large parts of the Indian party as well.

None of these, however, wished to become satellites of Peking, any more than did the other two Communist parties —Rumanian and Cuban—which also used the Sino-Soviet conflict to play off Moscow against Peking and increase their own independence.

THE RUMANIAN DEVIATION

The Rumanian party was anti-Russian because of the Soviet recovery of Bessarabia after World War II; because of the Latin, anti-Slav tradition of Rumanian culture; because of Russian infiltration and control of the party, since 1917, by largely ethnically non-Rumanian (Hungarian, Ukrainian, Bulgarian, Jewish) Communists; and because of Khrushchev's desire in the early 1960s to bring about an economically rational integration of Eastern Europe, which could only work to the disadvantage of such economically underdeveloped countries as Rumania. Since 1952 the party was in the hands of ethnically Rumanian nationalist elements led by Gheorghiu-Dej. Stalinist in internal policy (otherwise they could hardly have afforded to break with Moscow), they had long waited for an opportunity to assert their independence—and the Sino-Soviet split gave it to them.

Perhaps as early as 1954, certainly after the withdrawal of Soviet troops in 1958, the Rumanians maneuvered with Byzantine skill to slip almost imperceptibly out from under Moscow's hegemony so that by 1962 they had deviated from it—by adjusting their foreign trade pattern so as to balance Soviet trade with trade with the West (which would pay hard currency for Rumanian oil, grain, and timber), by maintaining neutrality in the Sino-Soviet dispute and by establishing correct, if not good, relations with *all* major powers. (Only with Budapest, their traditional enemy, because of Transylvania, were they—albeit not publicly—on bad terms.)

5

The 1962 Cuban Missile Crisis— and the End of the Berlin Crisis

While all these Sino-Soviet developments were under way—only partially, at the time, realized in the West—Soviet-American relations were in a new and paradoxical state: a combination of wish for détente and actions toward intensification of tension. Khrushchev wanted a Soviet-American détente, but, of course, on his own terms, which, he felt, should reflect what he saw as the shift in the world balance toward the Soviets. (He was the more determined to push back American power in order to refute the Chinese accusation that he was betraying the cause of world revolution.) In particular, the longer he postponed his "solution" of the situation in West Berlin—that is, an American surrender of its position there—the more he was determined to achieve it, without entering into serious risks of a thermonuclear confrontation with the still much superior United States. His hope that he could bring the United States to a peaceful retreat had been strengthened by the compromise of the new

American President, John F. Kennedy, in Laos (which seemed to Khrushchev at least to amount to a partition of the country) and, even more, by his impression of Kennedy at their confrontation in Vienna. He apparently thought that Kennedy was an opponent whom he could bluff into retreat.

Kennedy, on the other hand, also was following a double policy; he hoped to move toward a détente with Khrushchev, essentially for the same reason—to limit the risk of nuclear war—but at the same time he was determined not to back down in Berlin. In order to strengthen the overall American position he ordered a substantial increase in strategic and conventional capabilities, so that by 1962—in large part, it should be added, as a result of decisions taken under the Eisenhower Administration—American ICBM superiority over the Soviet Union was in the order of four to one. But super-power confrontations, as always throughout history, are not only objective—the actual balance of power—but subjective as well—each opponent's image of the other's capability and, more importantly, his will. Khrushchev clearly underestimated Kennedy's.

It is within this context that one must view the Cuban missile crisis of October 1962—*the* watershed of postwar international politics. It was so for two reasons: first, it glaringly revealed United States superiority over the Soviet Union, and second, it made equally clear the impotence of all other powers—the Chinese, the British, the French, and the Cubans, once a decisive strategic confrontation occurred.

CASTRO

Fidel Castro was—and is—primarily a charismatic, modernizing Latin American *caudillo*, or chief. His small guerrilla movement in the Sierre Maestre was made up primarily of young, radical, extreme nationalist intellectuals (or, better, "half-intellectuals") of middle-class background. His urban support was also middle-class; the Cuban Communists were anything but revolutionary and almost until the end they allied not with Castro but with Batista. Castro won not because of any mass revolutionary sentiment but because Batista's regime—corrupt, discredited, and top-heavy—collapsed.

After his 1959 victory, Castro was determined to retain absolute power and to carry out a social and economic revolution in Cuba and throughout Latin America. Since the United States opposed especially his Latin American and dictatorial aims, he followed an anti-American course. (This was quite natural: extreme Latin American nationalists are almost without exception anti-American, if only because United States power is so overwhelming.) He therefore almost inevitably turned toward America's great enemy, the Soviet Union, from which he got the economic aid to keep him going and from which he expected protection against United States intervention.

Eisenhower tried—too little, too late, too clumsily—to prevent Castro from moving toward Moscow, but even if he had made more concessions to the Cuban leader, it is most doubtful that he would have succeeded. The Russians were far from enchanted—and with considerable reason—by Castro's embrace; indeed, the Cuban dictator's 1961 proclamation that he was a Marxist-Leninist and "had always been one" (which was nonsense) failed to evoke any great enthusiasm from Khrushchev. But Castro outmaneuvered Khrushchev, who was in any case hardly in a position, given the Chinese threat, to refuse to assist a professed Communist leader, and who was undoubtedly also attracted to scoring a blow against the United States through supporting Fidel.

Castro's ambitions have always gone much further than Cuba; he saw himself as the new Bolívar (far more than the Marx) of all Latin America. He was convinced that guerrilla warfare would destroy the Latin American oligarchies as easily—or at least in the long run as surely—as it had Batista;

and one of his guerrilla associates, the Argentinian Ernesto "Che" Guevara, was even more committed than he to this Latin American strategy.

The United States was, of course, flatly opposed to Castro taking over Latin America, the more so once he had declared himself a Communist and a Soviet ally. What few Americans then realized, and far from all do yet, is that the picture was much more complex than just that: Khrushchev (and Brezhnev after him) were also far from enthusiastic about such a prospect. Remembering what had happened with Mao, they did not want to create another major Communist leader. However, in any case they were trapped between Castro on the one hand, whom they felt compelled to aid at least in Cuba, and the Latin American Communist leaders, who were pro-Soviet by tradition, now the more so, and the more valuable to Moscow because they, unlike Castro, preferred the peaceful, parliamentary road to power—more precisely, they preferred to struggle within, and if possible share the fruits of, the Latin American political system rather than to take to the hills as guerrillas.

When President Kennedy took office in early 1961, he was immediately confronted with one specific Cuban problem —what to do with the exile Cubans whom the United States Central Intelligence Agency had been training, at Eisenhower's instructions, in preparation for an overthrow of Castro. Faced with the necessity of either going through with or calling off the planned invasion, Kennedy, new in office, hesitated and tried to have it both ways: he neither called off the invasion nor gave it sufficient support to hold even a beachhead. The result, in April 1961, was the humiliating fiasco of the Bay of Pigs. Castro, triumphant, was, of course, fully confirmed in his view that the United States was his total and inveterate enemy. Khrushchev was probably further influenced to underestimate Kennedy's fundamental determination.

Kennedy drew several lessons from the fiasco: he did

not again accept his advisers' opinions without long and in-dependent questioning of them; he was more than ever deter-mined to launch a major multilateral program of economic aid and reform for Latin America (the Alliance for Progress); and he was also determined to prevent Castro from carrying out his program to win Latin America by guerrilla war. Hence, along with the Vietnam situation, Kennedy's great emphasis on counterinsurgency—the Special Forces ("Green Berets"). By his support for such left-wing, reformist leaders in Latin America as Betancourt in Venezuela and Frei in Chile, plus his emphasis on counter-guerrilla operations, Kennedy effectively contributed to domestic reform south of the border and at the same time toward checking Castro's aim of continental revolution through guerrilla war.

Fundamentally Latin America, like Eastern Europe, Southeast Asia, and Africa, was weak and divided, and re-sponded to, rather than seriously influenced, the world bal-ance of power. Castro's initial support to the south came in large part from Latin American radicals who were convinced that he had Soviet aid and protection, and that, therefore, for the first time since the 1930s and early 1940s (when such a radical *caudillo* as Peron was pro-Nazi, for the same anti-American reason), what they saw as the stifling pressure of American political and economic hegemony could success-fully be resisted. In this context as well, therefore, the Cuban confrontation of 1962 was a decisive one.

THE OCTOBER 1962 CUBAN MISSILE CRISIS

With respect to its causes, far from all the evidence is yet available. Why did Khrushchev put the missiles into Cuba? Was it his or Castro's initiative? What were their objectives? What would have been the result had the missiles not been removed?

To begin with Castro: certainly he wanted the Soviet missiles, as he wanted all other kinds of Soviet involvement in the island, thus making him more secure against American intervention, tying down the Soviets more on his side, and, almost surely, impeding if not reversing the Soviet-American trend toward détente, at least in the nuclear field—something which Castro feared might well eventually result in the Soviets sacrificing him for an overall agreement with Washington.

As for Khrushchev, his later explicit justification for putting in the missiles—to prevent an American invasion of the island—should not be taken very seriously. Kennedy did not intend, after the Bay of Pigs, to invade Cuba, and in fact, as Khrushchev must have realized, putting in the missiles would if anything make an American invasion more rather than less likely. It is much more probable that Khrushchev's motives related primarily to the general strategic balance between the United States and the Soviet Union and specifically to the Berlin crisis. True, he had the previous August, by permitting Ulbricht to put up the Wall, stopped the massive flight of refugees from East to West Germany and thereby at least temporarily stabilized the situation in East Germany. But his ambitions went further—to force the United States out of West Berlin, thereby destabilizing the West German political scene, greatly weakening NATO, and generally lowering United States prestige throughout the world. Strategically, the at least potential Soviet lead represented by Sputnik was by 1962, as a result of Kennedy's massive step up of strategic (and conventional) American power, rapidly being eroded; indeed, Moscow was falling quickly behind. Emplacement of MRBM's in Cuba would quickly and cheaply catch up with the United States again and administer such a shock and defeat to Washington that American concessions in Berlin and elsewhere would become far more probable.

Khrushchev misjudged the situation and—worse still—his opponent. Kennedy had no intention of backing down in Cuba. He had strategic nuclear superiority; he had overwhelming conventional superiority in the area; and his strategy of blockade ("quarantine") was exquisitely designed to force the burden of escalation on the Russians.

When it became clear, that fateful third week in October 1962, in the first potential superpower nuclear confrontation in history, that Kennedy would not only maintain his quarantine but bomb or invade the island if Khrushchev did not pull out his missiles, the Russian leader did so—humiliatingly, unilaterally (he ignored Castro's howls of protest and the Chinese shrieks of betrayal), and definitively.

THE IMPACT OF THE CUBAN MISSILE CRISIS

It was as though the fog obscuring the international scene had suddenly been blown away, and its features revealed. The United States was demonstrated to be what was then—and, as we shall see, still is—the more powerful of the two superpowers. The Soviet Union was demonstrated to be what it was—an essentially regional power, a superpower in the nuclear area only, and even there still inferior to the United States.

Kennedy's moderation in victory, his concern lest Khrushchev's face be unnecessarily damaged, showed true statesmanship and also increased American prestige. The sovereign disregard of the Russians for their allies, and notably for Castro, further tarnished their revolutionary, "proletarian internationalist" role. The Latin American radical nationalists suddenly realized that Moscow could not be depended upon against the United States, and that Castro's placing himself under Soviet protection and influence had only resulted in his being sold out at a moment of crisis—just as he might well be again, were it in Moscow's interest.

Castro became convinced of the same. Although there was little that he could immediately do about it, he was reinforced in his determination to wage guerrilla war in Latin America. Behind the screen of their sanctimonious support for Castro, the Chinese were delighted, since Soviet victory would have been defeat for themselves as well as for the United States, while Soviet defeat, in their view, served to confirm what they had always maintained: that Khrushchev would at all times sacrifice the interests of communism and revolution to an agreement with Washington.

The reverberations in Europe, although little realized at the time, were among the most important. For the East European Communists it represented a great blow to Soviet prestige. This was of special significance in Bucharest, where the Rumanian leader Gheorghiu-Dej, already locked in economic and political struggle with Khrushchev, seems to have been emboldened by the Soviet defeat to bring his struggle out into the open.

Reaction in France

More important was the impact on General de Gaulle. Since his return to power in 1958 he had been determined to get France out of Algeria and to restore it to a dominant position in Western Europe, thereby to an independent position in the world—which, for him, meant the end of predominant United States influence on the European continent. By 1959 his policies in this respect were clear; in retrospect there was little that Eisenhower, Kennedy, or Johnson could have done about it.

De Gaulle realized that he could only dominate Western Europe if he had primary influence over West Germany and if he kept the British out of the Common Market. The latter was relatively easy, by exercising the French veto over British membership. The former initially also looked promising, since Adenauer, then still in power in Bonn, was pro-French and since Kennedy's interest in a rapprochement with Khrushchev and his willingness to make some minor concessions in the Berlin crisis made the old chancellor—understandably—suspicious. De Gaulle cleverly played on this by supporting

Adenauer completely in his adamant attitude against the Russians during the Berlin crisis. Moreover, de Gaulle was one of the few European statesmen to pledge immediate and total support to Kennedy in the Cuban crisis—since he was aware of its danger and he disliked having Khrushchev stir up the possibility of a war in Europe over events in the Caribbean. But when Kennedy won there so decisively and Soviet prestige fell, de Gaulle concluded that for the near future at least Moscow was no longer a danger to French or, indeed, to West European security. On the other hand, the overwhelming American victory added to his determination to remove United States influence from Europe, since to his mind, accustomed to thinking in balance-of-power categories, the United States was the more dangerous to France the more powerful it became.

Thus the Cuban missile crisis and the United States victory in it contributed greatly to de Gaulle's decision to withdraw military integration from NATO, to concentrate on combatting American influence in Europe and, in the world, and —once his efforts to win Bonn away from Washington failed with Adenauer's successor, Erhard—to balance between West Germany and the Soviet Union, in the eventual hope of getting both American and Soviet troops out of the Continent. That would leave to France—Germany, non-nuclear, therefore inferior—the leading role there.

In terms of the forthcoming Franco-Soviet rapprochement, therefore, Khrushchev did salvage something from the shambles of his Cuban missile adventure—but in the last analysis not much. He knew well that de Gaulle was neither friend nor satellite nor even ally of the Soviet Union, but interested only in playing with Moscow for French purposes. Even so, however, in the years thereafter this proved to be a useful opening for a renewed Soviet political offensive in Western Europe, intended to capitalize on de Gaulle's anti-American policies and the general rising European feeling that the Soviet threat had greatly diminished and that the threat of American economic if not political hegemony was beginning to rise in its place.

THE END OF THE BERLIN CRISIS

Soviet policy has traditionally moved toward détente with the United States after Moscow has suffered a defeat. Having failed in its attempt to reverse the strategic balance, and thus to avert the rise in American superiority, there remained for Moscow only to make the best of its defeat by trying to make political capital out of it; that is, by returning to the time-tried tactic of "dividing the imperialists." The first result of the new Soviet shift toward détente was almost unnoticed, it was so quiet—the end of the Berlin crisis. Moscow simply stopped talking about Berlin and had Ulbricht do the same; and the crisis evaporated. The intimate connection between the Berlin and Cuban crisis was thereby clearly demonstrated. Nor as of this writing (1970) has the Berlin crisis resumed, in spite of signs from time to time that Ulbricht would like to set it going again. Soviet interest in preventing too great deterioration of United States-Soviet Union relations over the war in Vietnam, and, later, to prevent a renewed Middle East confrontation and to initiate strategic-arms-limitations talks, plus—a new factor—Russian fear lest a new Berlin crisis bring Washington, Paris, and Bonn together again, have combined to keep the divided city relatively quiet.

It would be wrong to think, however, that the West scored an unadulterated victory when the Berlin crisis ended in late 1962. The Berlin Wall has helped to stabilize East Germany; and the bitterness of the West Germans at not being able to visit or help their relatives and fellow Germans in East Germany has led to rising frustration, a growth in radical sentiment on the right and left, and a desire to see if concessions to Ulbricht might not help ameliorate the effects of the Wall. (It also led to a new Bonn policy toward the East altogether.)

By July 1963 the post-missile crisis détente also led to the signature of the partial test-ban treaty. This marked perhaps the height since 1945 of Soviet-American détente. It arose fundamentally from the common interest of Moscow and Washington in avoiding the risk of a nuclear war and, more specifically, in "closing the nuclear club"—preventing any more powers from gaining nuclear capability. Washington viewed this danger from a world perspective, and particularly with respect to the underdeveloped world: it was convinced that the spread of nuclear weapons, particularly to under-developed, unstable, radical regimes, could only heighten the danger of nuclear war. Moscow probably shares this concern, certainly with respect to China, but it is primarily concerned with preventing West Germany from having any access to nuclear weapons.

As it turned out the treaty was signed by almost all the powers, except Communist China, France, Cuba, Albania, North Vietnam, and North Korea. Peking and Paris already had nuclear capability; and for Paris, like Moscow, the treaty was essentially—and properly—directed against Bonn. (Only by keeping West Germany from going nuclear can France hope for hegemony in Western Europe.) Castro's refusal to sign was ostensibly a protest against American hostility toward him, as were the refusals by Hanoi and Pyongyang; but it was mainly on the part of all three a protest against Soviet-American détente and a desire to keep on reasonably good terms with Peking as well as with Moscow.

The Cuban missile crisis also encouraged Gheorghiu-Dej to make public, if only in a disguised form, his differences with Khrushchev and effectively to block economic integration of Eastern Europe through the Council of Mutual Economic Aid (CMEA). After probably trying and failing to change the Rumanian leadership, Khrushchev made the best of a bad bargain, and Dej pursued a deviationist nationalist course.

Brezhnev's modification of Khrushchev's policies toward Peking, by abandoning the former's opposition to Communist neutralism as between Moscow and Peking, naturally eased Moscow-Bucharest relations. Moreover, after Khrushchev had given up his attempts at economic integration of Eastern Europe and the Soviet Union, he *nolens volens* turned toward bilateral and multilateral agreements, especially among those states where Soviet influence remained the strongest—the so-called "northern tier," Poland, East Germany, and Czechoslovakia. Thus Rumania could the more easily continue her trade reorientation toward the West.

Bucharest also began expanding its diplomatic contacts with the West and the underdeveloped world, with the United States, West Germany, France, and Israel as well as with Yugoslavia. American and West German policy responded favorably to this move, leading in January 1967, over strong but unsuccessful opposition from Ulbricht, to the reestablishment of diplomatic relations between Bonn and Bucharest (the first East European state which took this step), as well as in April 1967 to a new, much-expanded trade agreement between Israel and Rumania. This was followed by Bucharest's refusal to copy Moscow's rigidly anti-Arab stand in June 1967, the third Israeli-Arab war.

Gheorghiu-Dej died in 1964. He was succeeded by the young, tough, nationalistic Nicolae Ceauşescu, who carried on Dej's policies, added some (but restricted) internal liberalization, notably in the security and economic fields, and made clear that he would agree with or differ from Soviet policies entirely from the viewpoint of Rumania's national interests—a position which further weakened Soviet prestige and influence, and which the West, and Peking, could only applaud.

THE SINO-SOVIET SPLIT

Sino-Soviet relations had been bad and getting worse before the Cuban crisis, but they worsened more rapidly and extensively thereafter. The Soviet surrender to United States pressure confirmed Mao in his view that Khrushchev was a traitor, and led the Chinese leader to hope that he could gain further support from other Communists and radical-nationalists, like Castro and Ho, whose anti-Americanism made them hold the same views. Moreover, at the same time as the Cuban missile crisis, in late October 1962, the Chinese had invaded the northern borders of India, in Ladakh and the Himalayas. After two weeks of uninterrupted success, in which they overwhelmed and humiliated the Indian units facing them, Peking suddenly called off the war.

The Indians had acted foolishly before the crisis. After having neglected his armed forces for years and shortsightedly having tried to appease the Chinese, under the influence of his defense minister Krishna Menon, Prime Minister Nehru had, the week before the Chinese struck, publicly called on the Indian Army to drive the Chinese out of the border posts they had occupied—and then had done nothing about it.

But this was for the Chinese only a pretext. Mao was determined to humiliate and to destroy Nehru politically, as well as to wreck Indian prestige and influence in the under-developed world. He largely succeeded. The Soviets, on the other hand, anxious lest they lose their influence in Delhi and leave the Indians under American influence, and determined to foist the aggressor label on the Chinese, strongly denounced Mao's course, thereby further worsening Sino-Soviet relations.

Even so, in early 1963, upon the urging of other relatively "neutral" Communist parties, Moscow and Peking agreed to hold bilateral talks in preparation for an international

Communist conference. But long before the talks began, in
Moscow in July 1963, simultaneously with the final negotiations there of the test-ban treaty, it had become clear that
this was all just shadowboxing: neither Khrushchev nor Mao
had any intention of coming to an agreement, but, on the
contrary, each was vowed to the other's defeat. The Sino-
Soviet talks in Moscow collapsed without any agreement and
the Chinese made quite clear publicly that they considered
Khrushchev and the Soviet leadership traitors to Marxism-
Leninism who should be deposed by the "Soviet workers."
Khrushchev, on the other hand, accused Mao of petty-bour-
geois nationalism, Trotskyism, and assorted other heinous de-
viations, and began again to attempt to mobilize all Communist parties throughout the world against the Chinese.

This Soviet attempt at anti-Chinese mobilization took the
form of summoning an international Communist conference,
where, on Moscow's initiative, Peking would be formally excommunicated and a coordinated worldwide campaign against
Chinese actions and influence would be launched—just as
Stalin had done in 1948 with the Cominform against Yugoslavia.

But Khrushchev, who in so many respects in domestic
affairs had successfully tried to shake off the worst of Stalin's
heritage, seemed unwilling or unable to do so as effectively
in his relations with the international Communist world. The
Yugoslav rebellion, de-Stalinization, the 1956 Polish and Hungarian events, the Chinese and Albanian defections, and finally
the Cuban defeat had so weakened Soviet prestige and influence that exactly the opposite occurred from what Khrushchev had wanted: not only did Khrushchev not achieve the
"collective mobilization" he strove for but in the process
of trying for it he lost still more prestige and influence. In
the process of negotiating—since he could no longer command
—such a mobilization, he had to make such concessions as
to its character and objectives to his reluctant and partial

allies—the Rumanians, Italians, Yugoslavs, and others—and even so was unable to persuade other, key parties, especially North Korea and North Vietnam, that the "mobilization" never took place. And each time he tried for it, the Soviet Union ended up less powerful than before.

6

The World of the
Mid- and Late-Nineteen Sixties

When one compares the world of 1970 with that of 1962, the two most striking, and the most paradoxical, new phenomena which the comparison presents, and those with the most significance for relations among the United States, Russia, and China, are, first, superiority of American power coupled with the crisis in American foreign and domestic affairs plus rising Soviet military power, and, second, the gradual, sometimes interrupted, but continuing, move toward Soviet-American détente, toward limitation of their conflict relationship. In order to understand these two processes, which were the background for the specific foreign policy problems of the late 1960s, something must first be said about their causes and consequences.

It had seemed in the late 1950s that Khrushchev might be right in his boast that by 1970 the Soviet Union would have caught up with and passed the United States. By the end of the 1960s it was clear that the contrary process had

been under way: overall United States superiority over the
Soviet Union was greater than in 1958, yet American purposes
and will in foreign policy were more in doubt. In what did
this superiority and crisis consist, and how and why had
they developed?

ECONOMIC AND TECHNOLOGICAL SUPERIORITY

American superiority was most of all economic and technological. Soviet growth rates fell, and those in the United
States nearly doubled, in the early and mid-1960s as compared to the preceding decade. In the case of the Soviet
Union, this reflected the maturing of the Russian industrial
society and the consequent slowing down of the growth
rate, plus, at least as importantly, several disastrous harvests,
which highlighted what seemed to be (primarily for political reasons—the continuation of agricultural collectivization)
the perennial backwardness and stagnation of Soviet agriculture. In the case of the United States, the post-1960 rise in
the annual growth rate resulted from the adoption by Kennedy, and the maintenance by Johnson and Nixon, of neo-
Keynesian counter-cyclical economic policies, which resulted
in years of unparalleled prosperity and rapid economic
growth.

This economic growth was coupled with technological
advance of a major nature—the entry of the United States
into the "post-industrial" age. Characterized by the intensive
and extremely extensive use of electronic computers and
other aspects of information technology which permitted
rapid automatizing (automation) of many industrial processes, the new technology produced for most of American
society consumer affluence of hitherto unknown proportions
—an immensely complex, rationalized, bureaucratic corporate
system. (It also contributed to the alienation of youth and
the American domestic crisis.) Moreover, it led to a thrust

abroad of United States corporate investment, ownership, and control, which particularly in Europe resulted in widespread fears of "American take-over"—what is known as the "technological gap." This gap, which arose as much from more effective American technological education and management as from technology and investment itself, was also felt in the Communist world—evidenced by East European purchases of American industrial computers, primarily because the Soviet Union was several years behind the United States in this field.

American technological superiority over the Soviet Union was most dramatically demonstrated in 1969 by the striking success of two American manned expeditions to the moon. The Soviet Union thus appeared to be at least temporarily considerably behind in the space race.

The American leap forward in industry, technology, and space was connected in part with new developments in military technology. After the Cuban crisis it had been felt by many Western experts that a plateau had been reached with respect to major innovations in the arms field and that the arms balance would at most change quantitatively, but hardly qualitatively, in the near future. Kennedy's rearmament measures increased American strategic superiority; and his conventional rearmament, plus the further impetus of United States involvement in Vietnam, increased American conventional strength as well. Conversely, Soviet defeats in Cuba and the Congo, and its relative inactivity in Vietnam, seemed to have confirmed its status as a regional power. By 1970, however, it was quite clear that those who had foreseen an arms plateau had reckoned without Moscow's answer to its Cuban defeat and also without the rush forward of technological innovation on both sides.

Khrushchev's fall, in October 1964, had occurred primarily for reasons of internal politics: his increasing impatience with, and attempts to surround and override, his colleagues. His failures in foreign policy, against the Chinese and even in the Cuban missile crisis, played a secondary role, and Soviet foreign policy displayed basic continuity thereafter.

The Arms Race

Khrushchev's successors, even more than he, were un-prepared—as Stalin had been after 1945—to accept permanent United States strategic and conventional superiority. (Conversely, the United States has been until recently unwilling to accept strategic parity with the Soviet Union; and these two conflicting policies, plus verification problems, have formed the basic cause of the continuing Russian-American arms race.) By 1970, through a crash program of ICBM deployment, the Soviets had brought down the American strategic lead from four to one to somewhere near parity, and were perhaps, because of their larger rockets, even at or above parity in actual megatonnage. (This was counterbalanced by the relatively more invulnerable—"harder"—American strategic weapons systems such as the undersea Polaris.) Moreover, the Soviets began a substantial program of building up conventional weapons, notably a five-ocean navy and long-range air- and sea-lift capacity, the lack of which had been such a handicap to them in Cuba, the Congo, and Vietnam. This included the reestablishment of an amphibious marine corps and a major, continuing increase in naval forces, including construction of helicopter attack carriers, plus deployment of an important Soviet fleet in the Mediterranean. Finally, in the field of active strategic ballistic missile defense (BMD), the Soviets began to deploy around Moscow an antiballistic missile system (ABM), designed to cut down destruction from an American strategic attack. For all these reasons, plus aid to North Vietnam, Soviet defense expenditures began to rise fairly rapidly.

At the same time Communist China had been pursuing its own nuclear program, after the setback at the beginning of the 1960s, as a result of the withdrawal of Soviet aid. Western experts estimated that by the early 1970s the Chinese could have medium-range nuclear missiles with delivery capability over East, South, and Southeast Asia, and by the mid-1970s their ICBMs could hit the United States as well.

The Soviet ABM and the later American ABM system were themselves major signs of the new escalatory cycle in weapons technology. By far the most significant technological leap forward in the arms race, however, one comparable only to ICBM deployment itself, was the American announcement in late 1967 of the decision to deploy a new weapons system, "multiple independently targeted reentry vehicles" (MIRV). This involves several warheads in one missile, which upon approaching the target divide and rush toward different targets. They are much more effective, because they are much more accurate, in "deliverable megatonnage" than are equivalent single warheads; they pose much greater problems for active defense; and they will greatly increase the United States "assured destruction" capability. (It is assumed that the Soviets are somewhat behind the United States on MIRV, but somewhat ahead on ABM.)

President Johnson proposed, ostensibly against the mid-1970s ICBM Chinese threat, the deployment of the "thin" SENTINEL ABM system, which would protect United States cities and missile sites against Chinese, but not against Soviet, strategic capabilities. President Nixon's SAFEGUARD system reduced this to protection of missile sites only, but against Soviet as well as Chinese capabilities. In mid-1970, American deployment of this ABM system had begun.

It is still too early to measure all the consequences of this new leap forward in the arms race, but it is already clear that they will be great. These are some of the consequences.

First, mobile missiles plus MIRV deployment by one or both sides will greatly decrease the possibility of effective reconnaissance; that is, of one side knowing the number, location, and capabilities of the other's strategic forces. (This had been much greater than commonly thought in the 1960s, because of the development by Washington and Moscow of very effective artificial satellite photography.) The deployment of these two new weapons systems will thus have a destabilizing effect because each side will have to deploy greater capability in order to be sure of at least parity.

Second, MIRV plus ABM will make much less effective the strategic forces of the smaller nuclear powers—China, France, and Great Britain—since they will probably not be able financially and technologically to deploy ABM or MIRV; Europe because it is not united and is unwilling to spend the money, and China because it is too underdeveloped. These small forces will therefore lose almost all of the little credibility they still have vis-à-vis the United States and the Soviet Union. Some of these powers will maintain their nuclear capability even so, but directed against non-nuclear powers: China against India and Japan; France against the possibility of a resurgent hostile Germany and in order to compensate for German economic superiority.

Third, because of the arms spiral, the two superpowers will become not only militarily but also technologically further superior to the rest of the developed world—to say nothing of the underdeveloped world as well. For the side benefits ("spin-off") of such technologically and especially electronically complex developments as MIRV and ABM are great. The United States, with its governmental-industrial-university complexes such as Cambridge and Los Angeles, rapidly and completely puts this spin-off to work in civilian industries. The Soviet Union clearly does not do it so rapidly or so efficiently, presumably because of secrecy and compartmentalization in its military as opposed to its civilian industries— a phenomenon not found in the United States, where the same corporations do both military and civilian business. This spin-off will be available only slowly and incompletely to the other developed nations.

All in all, then, both military and civilian developments will increase the technological gap between the United States and the rest of the developed world; will probably result in further expansion of American corporations' ownership and control of foreign industries, particularly in Western Europe; and will, thereby, raise the level of frustration and, therefore, of anti-American sentiments in many foreign countries—political developments which the Soviets can only view with favor. On the other hand, this will hardly be a universal phenomenon: those smaller countries such as the Benelux states and Italy, will, like Canada, prefer the rise in their standard of living which these developments will produce. They will therefore be less concerned than Great Britain, West Germany, and France about political and economic independence, and competition with the superpowers, since they are more concerned about avoiding domination by their stronger neighbors or by the Soviet Union than by the far-away United States.

SOVIET-AMERICAN DÉTENTE

The new technological leap forward in the arms race also strengthened the second main trend in the post-1962 world—the intensification of Soviet-American détente. This did not mean that Moscow and Washington developed anything like an alliance against China. On the contrary, they remained fundamentally in conflict. But the overriding danger of destructive thermonuclear war, symbolized and made emotionally compelling by the 1962 Cuban missile crisis, pushed the two superpowers steadily thereafter toward a series of measures to limit their conflict relationship. The first major step in this process was the 1963 partial test-ban treaty. The second was the 1967 non-proliferation treaty, which by the end of the decade had been ratified by most, but not all, of the world's states. The third, and in the long run perhaps the most significant, was the opening in 1969 of strategic-arms-limitation talks (SALT) between the United States and the Soviet Union.

This trend toward Soviet-American détente was sometimes interrupted, most recently by the August 1968 Soviet
invasion of Czechoslovakia, but it always resumed. Both Washington and Moscow pursued it despite the objections of their
allies, who feared that their interests would be sacrificed
without their being consulted and who disliked the superpowers' desire to prevent them from becoming significant
atomic powers. This was most of all true for the Soviet Union,
whose worsening relations with China were made more so
by its arms control negotiations with the United States. It
was also true, although less so, for Washington, some of
whose difficulties in the mid- and late-1960s with Paris and
Bonn reflected the same problem. By the end of the decade
the high cost and destabilizing danger of the new technological
cycle in the arms race had intensified the Soviet-American
interest in arms control and had contributed greatly to the
opening of SALT.

Within the context of these two major developments—
the rise of American economic and technological power and
the Soviet-American détente—we may now consider the main
developments of the late 1960s involving the United States,
Russia, and China.

THE CHINESE CULTURAL REVOLUTION

The first main development of the late 1960 s, and even
now the least understood, was the domestic convulsion in
China called the Cultural Revolution. In part as a result of
it, by the end of the decade Communist Chinese foreign
policy had suffered such a series of defeats abroad that Peking
had lost much of its international prestige and power. (Conversely, the Soviet Union's position in Communist states and
parties had significantly improved.)

Only recently did the world outside China begin to grasp
the extent, the intensity, and the significance of the factional
struggle in Chinese Communist society. This struggle went

much further back than it had seemed when it broke out in the open in 1966: indeed, it seems likely that Mao (with his main associate, Defense Minister Lin Piao) and his chief opponents—his deputy Liu Shao-ch'i, the party secretary-general Teng Hsiao-p'ing, the mayor of Peking P'eng Chen, and the army chief of staff Lo Jui-ch'ing (not all united on all issues) —had since 1957 been with increasing intensity disputing, struggling, and finally fighting to the finish about the whole range of foreign and domestic policy issues.

Their differences may be best summarized under three headings: domestic priorities, policy toward the Soviet Union, and policy toward the United States. With respect to the first, Mao was determined to bring about industrialization, collectivization, and, above all, a massive change in the society and the collective and individual personality of China, by ideological and revolutionary fervor rather than by economic incentives, and to give these objectives priority over all other considerations, foreign and domestic. His opponents apparently felt (we know only Mao's—undoubtedly distorted —version of their views), for varying reasons, that such fanatical emphasis on ideology and revolutionary change would be counter-productive. As for the Soviet Union, the party functionaries, Liu and Teng at least, seem to have preferred a partial rapprochement with Moscow in order to get more Soviet aid for economic development, as did Lo in order to get military, particularly atomic, assistance. With respect to the United States, Lo seems to have felt that in general, and particularly in view of American escalation in Vietnam, China must view Washington rather than Moscow as the main enemy, and therefore get Soviet aid in order to defend China successfully against a feared United States attack, while taking greater risks vis-à-vis Washington in order to aid Hanoi. Mao and Lin Piao, on the other hand, believed that the Soviet Union, not the United States, was the main enemy, and that, therefore, China should not risk American intervention in North Vietnam or against the Chinese mainland, but should rather take a lower-risk posture against Washington, urge Hanoi to return from "main-force" to guerrilla warfare, and concentrate on the struggle against Moscow.

In any case, Mao became convinced in 1960-61, after the failure of the Great Leap Forward, that China was menaced by a post-revolutionary turn toward moderation, and also that, rather than going along with this, one must fight it by means of much more extreme policies. These included a massive purge of the party apparatus, which he saw as becoming increasingly bureaucratized, subject to local and functional differentiation, and returning, after the revolutionary spasm, to something dangerously like a normal routine.

When in 1965 Mao met strong, perhaps majority, opposition, he decided to get around it by using his "palace guard" (including his wife and his secretary) to push aside the party leadership, which he did by summer of 1966 by relying much more heavily upon the (also purged) army, and by mobilizing youthful, fanatical activists, (the Red Guard) to fight—often literally—the party functionaries in Peking and throughout the country.

The result in 1966 and 1967 was near-chaos throughout China. Army, Red Guards, and party functionaries fought hand-to-hand in some cities. Even after Mao retreated to a compromise solution involving the reintegration of some of the party functionaries in a new "three-group" system of revolutionary committees, only in late 1968 did he reestablish something like control of all China. Economic activity declined, exports slumped badly, and the morale, dynamism, and conviction of success on the part of Chinese communism was seriously affected. Yet, by the April 1969 party congress, he, and even more his designated successor Lin Piao, seemed to be again at the helm.

In foreign policy, the Cultural Revolution brought intensified extremism as well, in particular by drastically worsening Sino-Soviet relations. From 1966 to 1969, anti-Soviet sound and fury in China, in part the result of spontaneous mass xenophobia, reached unparalleled heights. The Soviet Embassy in Peking was beleaguered in early 1966; Soviet diplomats were beaten up; and reports increased of Chinese provocations on the frontier with the Soviet Union—insults to Soviet border troops and Chinese troop mobilizations there. Most seriously, in early 1969 there were two severe Sino-Soviet border clashes on the Ussuri River, on the boundary between Manchuria and the Soviet Maritime Province, with many killed and wounded. They seem to have probably been instigated by the Chinese. (In June 1969 there was another in Sinkiang, very likely Soviet-inspired.)

Mao also in effect took over what the Soviets had abandoned with Khrushchev's fall: the attempt at "collective mobilization," this time of the "Communist neutrals" against the Soviets. But his efforts to force his hitherto semi-allies to line up fully with him against Brezhnev backfired badly: North Vietnam returned to a careful neutrality; North Korea became more anti-Chinese than anti-Soviet; Cuba refused to ally with China; and in the September 1965 fall of Sukarno in Indonesia, China suffered a major diplomatic disaster.

Until September 1965, when coup and counter-coup in Djakarta revolutionized Indonesia's political scene, China had enjoyed the support, as a junior ally, of Sukarno and the powerful Indonesian Communist party (PKI). Then, whether started by the PKI, young rebellious officers, Sukarno, or all three, most of the army's top generals (the army had been the PKI's great opponent) were killed in a coup, but two—Nasution and Suharto—by chance escaped. Suharto then took over, gradually nudged Sukarno out of power, tolerated if not encouraged the mass slaughter whereby hundreds of thousands of Indonesian Communists were massacred, and turned away from China—and Russia as well—toward a mildly pro-Western policy, if only to get the economic aid to repair Indonesia's shattered economy, wrecked by Sukarno's dilettantism and foreign policy ambitions. Thus, China's foreign policy suffered an immense blow, in Southeast Asia and in the underdeveloped world in general.

As the Cultural Revolution proceeded, Mao became also increasingly extremist toward his hitherto friendly neighbors —including Burma, Cambodia, and Nepal—but only with negative results. By mid-1969, with the exception of tiny Albania in the Mediterranean and of small, nearly impotent Communist splinter groups around the world, China's influence was limited to its own boundaries. Yet, by mid-1970 Mao, Lin, and Chou En-lai were slowly beginning to reactivate Peking's foreign policy, which during the Cultural Revolution had been in fact nearly paralyzed. It was too early, though, to tell what this would bring.

In any case, China entered the 1970s a weak, underdeveloped power. Japan was potentially the major power in Asia. America's agreement in 1969 to return Okinawa to Japan, plus the reelection of the pro-American Liberal Democrats, seemed to consolidate Japanese-American relations. Conversely, although Moscow seemed increasingly desirous of cultivating Tokyo, Japanese desires to recover the Kurile Islands from the Soviet Union made this process more difficult.

THE VIETNAM WAR AND THE CRISIS OF THE AMERICAN POLITY

The second of the major foreign developments was the Vietnam War, which in the late 1960s increasingly overshadowed American foreign and domestic policy. The United States slid into it under three Presidents—Eisenhower, Kennedy, and Johnson—without having realized its cost in men, money, and domestic division. By 1968, the war seemed stymied, with more than one-half million U. S. troops in Vietnam and no end to the war in sight, but with the Sino-Soviet split and the increasingly neutral position of Hanoi in it having removed much of the initial basis for American intervention—to contain "Asian communism." In March 1968 President Johnson decided to reverse American policy and cease the bombing of North Vietnam, in the hope of a negotiated settlement, while simultaneously bowing out of the Presidential campaign. The victor in it—Nixon—expanded Johnson's policy shift to include graduated American disengagement, at least of combat troops, and "Vietnamization" of the war. Meanwhile, domestic dissent over the war, which had reached new heights under Johnson, appeared to decline somewhat as a result of these policy reversals, but remained a serious problem for American policy makers.

The Vietnam dissent contributed greatly to a rise in the United States of a new radicalism. Largely university-and student-based, but reflecting increasing public concern about the failure to win in Vietnam and such domestic problems as civil rights, poverty, education, and the black urban ghettos, by 1969 American radicals were deeply involved in an attempt by the American left to limit commitments abroad and transfer large sums from the defense budget to meet domestic problems. More generally, the United States was increasingly seen by many Americans, and even more by the rest of the world, as a nation caught in a spiral of divisive domestic crises which might well paralyze its foreign and its domestic policy. Although this seemed improbable, and although the new Nixon Administration, while reflecting traditional Republican concentration on Western Europe and Japan rather than the third world, seemed unlikely to carry out a decisive worldwide American withdrawal, it did seem by 1970 that Washington would be limiting rather than increasing its overseas commitments. How this would interact with the rush forward at home and abroad of American technology and industry remained to be seen.

For the Soviet Union, the Vietnam War was a major gain. First, the war tied down American forces and spent American money, thus making United States action against

Soviet interests elsewhere less likely. Second, it worsened Sino-American relations, a Soviet interest ever since the Sino-Soviet rift began. Third, it made the United States often attempt to get Soviet aid to end it, thus improving Moscow's position vis-à-vis Washington. Fourth, perhaps most importantly, it enabled Moscow to improve its position throughout the world, as a result of the increasing unpopularity of America's Vietnam policies, and in particular among Asian Communist parties—above all, North Vietnam and North Korea. This was true for two reasons: first, only the Soviet Union could—and did—provide the high-technology weapons (anti-aircraft guns and others) which Hanoi had to have once the American bombing began, and which Pyongyang needed against what it saw as an American threat. Second, after Khrushchev's fall Mao had not only begun to insist that all Communist parties line up against Moscow but also harassed Soviet weapons shipments across China to North Vietnam. Finally, Moscow successfully capitalized on Asian fear of Chinese expansion in East and Southeast Asia, notably in India, and in 1969 proposed an Asian security system clearly directed against Peking. (However, in early 1970 Cambodian developments helped Peking more than Moscow.)

Mao seems to have thought at first that the United States intervention in Vietnam foreshadowed an American invasion of China, and he clearly wanted Hanoi to fight to the last Vietnamese. Yet, Peking's policy, as opposed to its words, remained cautious, and increasingly centered on the threat from the Soviet Union rather than from the United States.

SINO-SOVIET RELATIONS

Thus, all the developments in the late 1960s contributed toward the continued worsening of Sino-Soviet relations. They reached their lowest point in early and mid-1969 with the two Sino-Soviet border incidents, along the Ussuri River and in Sinkiang. These incidents reflected an apparent Chinese intent to continue to harass the Soviet border (as demonstrated, probably, by the Ussuri incident) and a firm intent of the Soviet Union to prevent this (as shown, probably, by the Sinkiang clash). The Soviets felt compelled to move large forces to the Chinese border; and indeed, their increasing concern with the Chinese may well have contributed to their desire for détente with the United States (via SALT) and in Europe (via their European Security Conference proposal). There were ominous signs in summer 1969 that at least some military circles in Moscow were contemplating some kind of military move against the Chinese, and these probably contributed to the Chinese willingness to begin low-level negotiations with the Soviets in late 1969 on the border situation. Yet, by mid-1970 these negotiations appeared to have made little progress, and the future of Sino-Soviet relations appeared black, indeed.

The new Nixon Administration was, carefully and very gradually, undertaking to improve American relations with Peking. Moscow was understandably most apprehensive about this prospect, which in any case, if only because of such untractable issues as Taiwan, did not seem likely to materialize too rapidly. Nevertheless, the American initiatives did reflect Washington's desire to remain neutral between its two major antagonists and, although it of course denied it, thus to profit from their differences.

As Sino-Soviet relations worsened, China came to be seen by the rest of the world as in the grip of fanaticism and xenophobia, and as the Vietnam War gave it new opportunities, Moscow made some progress, albeit probably only temporarily, in improving its position in the Communist world. After Khrushchev's fall in October 1964, his successors, Brezhnev and Kosygin, abandoned the former's attempt to force all Communist parties into an anti-Chinese front. They proceeded much more cautiously and flexibly, *inter alia* by giving military support to North Vietnam and North Korea and not objecting to their neutrality between Moscow and Peking. (China, conversely, during the Cultural Revolution became so fanatical in its demands for total support that Hanoi and Pyongyang moved away from its orbit.) After several false starts and an interruption due to their August 1968 invasion of Czechoslovakia, the Soviets finally succeeded in holding an international Communist conference at Moscow in June 1969. The meeting was, however, so characterized by open differences of opinion that its net result was to strengthen still further pluralistic tendencies and thus eventually still further weaken the Soviet position in the Communist world. Moreover, the 1970 reactivation of, and greater flexibility in, Chinese foreign policy enabled Peking to make some gains in North Korea and Indochina.

SOVIET-AMERICAN COMPETITION: THE MIDDLE EAST

By 1970 the Middle East was again close to war, after an initial respite subsequent to the decisive 1967 Israeli defeat of the Arabs. The successful Soviet forward policy in the Middle East reflected a combination of traditional Russian expansionism plus Communist ideological commitment to aid to revolutions. America was caught between its desire to ensure Israel's security and its oil and other interests in the conservative Arab states. The Arab states remained disunited; radicalism and, therefore, Soviet influence seemed to be rising in them; and American influence continued to decline. Yet, Israel remained superior militarily to the Arabs, and only the United States could get the Israelis out of the Arab territories they had conquered in 1967. Even so, Moscow's early 1970 introduction of Soviet pilots into Egypt, in response to Israeli raids near Cairo, threatened a Soviet-Israeli, and thereafter a Soviet-American, confrontation. The August 1970 American-sponsored truce seems at this writing (November 1970) far from a good bet to endure indefinitely, and the recent bloody civil war in Jordan and Nasser's death make successful negotiations even more unlikely.

Washington and Moscow seemed only to agree on preventing the worsening Middle Eastern situation from entangling them in a Soviet-American confrontation, but otherwise to remain in conflict in the area, with Moscow winning. China was still too weak and far away to play a significant role in the area.

THE THIRD WORLD

For a time in the 1950s and early 1960s the underdeveloped third world had profited much from competition for its political support, through military and economic aid, by Washington, Moscow, and Peking. Its votes in the United Nations General Assembly plus the general optimism about its prospects, particularly in the United States, made it seem quite powerful. By 1970, however, this was seen by most to have been at best a dream and at worst a delusion.

Firstly, what little unity the third world ever had was gone, largely a victim of Soviet-United States, Chinese-United States, and, above all, Sino-Soviet competition. Secondly, the "terms of trade," that is, the relationship of the raw materials sold by the third world as compared to the manufactured products they buy from the developed world, during the last decade changed greatly to the third world's disadvantage and to the advantage of the developed countries—so much so, in fact, as to outweigh all the economic aid given to the third world. Moreover, all the efforts by the third world, notably by the United Nations Conference on Trade and Development (UNCTAD), to compensate for this, have so far been unsuccessful. The enormous leap forward of agricultural productivity in the developed countries, notably in the United States and Canada, further worsened the underdeveloped countries' position. All in all, therefore, economics added to politics to worsen the position of the third world.

Thirdly, the population explosion, the lack of economic development, and the political crises and military coups which ever more frequently plagued the third world made its prestige and, therefore, its weight in international affairs decline considerably more. Chinese efforts, particularly in Africa, have as yet come to little or nothing, essentially because Peking has been too ignorant, too arrogant, and too little concerned about the interests of the African states. Soviet-American competition in much of the underdeveloped world had also declined somewhat in force and extent, in large part because both Washington and Moscow came to realize that there was little to be gained out of it for either of them. India was rent with internal dissension; the United Arab Republic was defeated; Indonesia exchanged Sukarno for domestic consolidation; Ben Bella and Nkrumah were overthrown. All in all, most underdeveloped countries were more concerned with their internal problems than with foreign policy.

EASTERN EUROPE

In Eastern Europe, where Moscow could use Red Army tanks to maintain its key positions and was prepared to do so even at the cost of interfering with Soviet-American détente, Soviet control, with the exception of Yugoslavia, Rumania, and Albania, continued to be predominant. For a time it seemed threatened in Czechoslovakia. Beginning in 1962 and intensifying strongly after the replacement of the Stalinist Novotný by Alexander Dubček at the beginning of 1968, a wave of liberalization swept through Czechoslovakia, similar to what had occurred in Poland and Hungary in 1956. Although the Czechoslovak Communist party remained in general control of events, and Prague neither left the Warsaw Pact nor dissolved the Communist party, as Nagy had felt compelled to do in Budapest in 1956, the Soviet leadership—convinced that the repercussions of Czechoslovak liberalization menaced their vital interests in Poland, East Germany, and even the Soviet Union itself—invaded Czechoslovakia in August of that year.

The invasion, contrary to Budapest in 1956, went off without resistance. Although initially Dubček and his associates, after being arrested and mistreated, were returned by Moscow to office, and seemed for some months to have saved at least part of the "Prague Spring," this proved to be an illusion. After Dubček was replaced by Gustav Husák in April 1969, repression rapidly intensified in Czechoslovakia, and by 1970 Prague was under a more repressive tyranny than the, by then, partially liberalized Budapest.

Yet, the Soviets had recoiled before sending their armies into Rumania or Yugoslavia, both because liberalization had not gone so far there and because Washington had made clear to Moscow that any such moves would gravely endanger Soviet-American détente. The Soviet invasion of Czechoslovakia could best be understood, like the crushing by the Tsars of the nineteenth-century Polish rebellions, as an expression of Russian imperial will. Nevertheless, none of the problems of Eastern Europe, above all, its technological backwardness, were solved by it.

SOVIET-AMERICAN COMPETITION: WESTERN EUROPE

One reason, although not the primary one, why the Soviets had invaded Czechoslovakia was their fear that their declining influence there would be replaced by West Germany. The "new German Eastern policy," begun under Chancellor Erhard, intensified under his successor Kiesinger, and pushed even more by Brandt, who became chancellor in late 1969, reflected the desire of West Germany to convert its affluent economy into political power so as to extend Bonn's influence in Eastern Europe, improve relations with Moscow, and ease the conditions of life in East Germany. (The United States, conversely, supported it, since it was in accord with Washington's own policies.) Moscow increasingly opposed this in 1967 and 1968, since it feared that this new policy would endanger its hold over East Germany and its influence in Eastern Europe. Yet, by 1970, with the Soviet hold over Eastern Europe reconsolidated by the invasion of Czechoslovakia, with the East European economies and the Soviet economy as well in increasing need of West German technology and credits, and with Brandt taking a more conciliatory position toward the East, Moscow modified its hostility and signed a treaty with Bonn which improved Soviet-German relations. (In late 1970 its ratification hinged on Soviet concessions on Berlin.)

This took place within the context of a more general revival of a forward Soviet strategy toward Western Europe, in particular, of the Soviet initiative for a European Security Conference. The Soviet purpose, as with the Rapacki Plan in the 1950s, was to consolidate its hold over Eastern Europe, obtain international recognition for East Germany, and lower American influence in Western Europe, as well as to overcome the remnants of what had been a brief and ineffective wave of Western indignation over Moscow's invasion of Czechoslovakia. American response to the Soviet European Security Conference reflected two conflicting tendencies: a desire not to reject it completely as a means of East-West détente, overridden for the present by fears that it would only weaken NATO. By 1970, this Soviet proposal had become an increasingly important factor in European politics.

Finally, like the United States, the Soviet Union had increasingly serious domestic problems, though they were less visible. Intellectual ferment had reached a level unprecedented in Soviet history; discontent among the minority nationalities (Ukrainians, Central Asians, and others) was on the rise; the Soviet economy remained sluggish; and the Soviet leadership seemed divided, bureaucratic, and unoriginal in its responses to these challenges, preferring police force to reform. Yet, Moscow's rule hardly seemed in decisive danger; rather, the outlook was for a continuation of bureaucratized, authoritarian communist rule.

Predictions are best left to soothsayers. They are hardly a useful task for contemporary historians. Yet, one projection may be safely ventured: the interaction between the three states which this book has treated—the United States, Russia, and Communist China—will more than any other factor determine the international politics of the 1970s.

Index